meatballs and matzah balls

Recipes and Reflections from a Jewish and Italian Life

MORE THAN 100 CLASSIC AND
NEW JEWISH AND ITALIAN RECIPES

Bum appetito and beté avon!
Marcia Friedman

by Marcia A. Friedman

Elsa Jacob Publishing | Ashburn, Virginia

For Daryl

Meatballs and Matzah Balls: Recipes and Reflections from a Jewish and Italian Life

Text, Recipes, and Photography by Marcia A. Friedman

Published by Elsa Jacob Publishing
Ashburn, Virginia

www.meatballsandmatzahballs.com
info@meatballsandmatzahballs.com

ISBN: 978-0-9886121-0-5

Book design and layout by Lucy Pope, 202design, www.202design.com

Printed in the United States of America

Contents

Introduction

Sometimes food is more than just something to eat. For me, anyway, it is also memories, culture, bonds, creativity, and connections. I think that's why I gravitated to getting to know Jewish food when I converted to Judaism more than 15 years ago. Making and enjoying the food and sharing it with others seemed like a touchstone for a new people and culture.

As I started exploring Jewish foods, though, my love of the meatballs and lasagna I grew up with kept tugging on my apron strings, returning me to my Italian heritage. As I was bringing something new to the table, the old called out to be revisited and explored beyond the beloved greatest hits of my well-assimilated Italian side. I had to take measure of that. And so I had myself a project—to build a repertoire of Jewish and Italian recipes, but Italian recipes that work in a kosher context (no small undertaking given all the rules).

Where to begin? How about the Jewish recipes of Ashkenazi (Eastern European) origin? That's where my future husband's family hailed from, and I was already familiar with these Jewish deli stand-bys such as latkes, matzah balls, and brisket. And while the recipe versions themselves interested me, so did the surrounding stories and arguments about the density of matzah balls, for example, or the variations on latkes and fried matzah. Who knew? Meanwhile, I delved into the volumes written on Italian food. From there, it didn't take long to uncover several collections of recipes passed down from Italy's small but vibrant Jewish community—an unexpected jackpot of ideas bridging the cultures and blazing a trail for Italian dishes adjusted to kosher rules. And then there was the natural trans-Mediterranean connection of Italy and the Jewish homeland of Israel, providing a whole other source of recipe ideas. Plus, I quickly learned that Jewish and Italian cuisines share some versions of essentially the same foods—like blintzes and crespelle, kreplach and ravioli, and Mandelbrot and biscotti.

Before I knew it, I became the kid in the candy store, delighted, slightly overwhelmed, and ready to indulge in all the possibilities. Time to start picking and choosing, cooking and testing. I wanted dishes for the Jewish holidays, family get-togethers, parties, and everyday meals. That meant classics from both traditions, recipes that incorporated features of both, and my own special creations that connected through history, ingredients, people, or in other ways big or small, to Italian, Jewish, or Mediterranean cuisine. As a home cook, all around I looked for appealing recipes and preparations that could be made in a regular kitchen and for a variety of tastes—and, of course, could be made kosher.*

Wanting each recipe to be sensational, successful, and something that I would want to make over and over again, I tested and re-tested. Recipes weren't "done" until I liked the results. This took a very long time, but produced recipes that have become some of my most treasured and requested, and anyone can enjoy them. I feel so possessive of them that I almost hesitate to give them out. Almost. This labor of love was to create a unique collection for me, but also to share.

Beyond the cooking and eating, this whole adventure with Jewish and Italian food bubbled over throughout with memories and meaning—about people, stories, culture, tradition, and how I related to it all. And so each chapter offers an essay highlighting a point or two on my cultural-culinary journey. Although not chronological and not essential to appreciating the recipes, these vignettes are best read in sequence. But as an avid cookbook reader myself, I know part of the fun is jumping in with whatever captures your interest most—and feel free to do that here.

So then, welcome to my Jewish-Italian kitchen. I truly hope that you enjoy these recipes and that at least some become favorites. In Italian, Yiddish, and Hebrew—*Buon appetito, est gezunterhayt, and bete'avon!*

*To help with kosher cooking, recipes are marked as dairy, meat, or pareve (neutral, neither meat nor dairy). For more on kosher requirements, see page 168.

Chapter 1

Soups and Stews

Come on in! If a food could hang a welcome sign on itself, soup would do it. Its roles as starter courses and comfort foods, and its ability to feed a crowd (especially the stews), make this group of recipes a friendly lot. At the heart is chicken soup, long in the first-aid arsenal of Jewish mothers and caretakers everywhere and a building block of many recipes—Jewish, Italian, or otherwise. My title recipe, meatball matzah balls, appears in this chapter, as do adaptations of such traditional stews as beef stew, sauerkraut, and chili. The chapter also includes the Jewish specialty matzah ball soup and the Italian vegetable soup minestrone. It also features one of my all-time favorites, a savory butternut squash soup sprinkled with toasted seeds.

Reflections
SCATTERED SEEDS

Recipes
ROASTED BUTTERNUT SQUASH SOUP

TOASTED SQUASH SEEDS

MEATBALL MATZAH BALLS
(MY JEWISH-ITALIAN DUMPLINGS)

GOOD OLD CHICKEN STOCK

CHICKEN NOODLE SOUP

HOMEMADE NOODLES FOR CHICKEN SOUP

CHILI (MARCIA'S CHOLENT)

MATZAH BALL SOUP

MINESTRONE

SAUERKRAUT WITH WHITE WINE
AND KOSHER SAUSAGE

JEWISH-ITALIAN BEEF STEW (HAMMIN)

ROASTED POTATOES FOR BEEF STEW

Scattered Seeds

My mom Sandra loved to try new recipes. One day she stood at the kitchen counter where she always worked and unfolded a piece of paper with handwritten instructions. She moved about the long narrow kitchen, gathering flour, salt, eggs, a packet of yeast, her well-worn wooden board, and her favorite slate blue glass mixing bowl. I stood at the counter, my nose and eyes a good height to observe her latest culinary adventure.

Soon my mom turned out a plump warm dough on her wooden board and began kneading. Even as an elementary school kid, I loved watching her and helping, and she encouraged my brother and me to become comfortable with food and cooking. She sent us to the backyard garden to pick the ripest tomatoes and pull spring onions from the earth. She stood back and let me experiment with my first original recipe, a beef noodle soup made with bouillon, wide egg noodles, and a bit too much black pepper. When it came to making meatballs for spaghetti sauce, she taught me how to mix the ingredients and roll the balls. As she worked on her bread, she turned the dough over to me to let me wrestle with it a few minutes, pushing and pressing and pulling to activate the yeast before setting the dough aside to rise.

I didn't realize how this bread was "different" until nearly two hours later. My mom took the swollen dough and divided it into pieces, which she rolled into long strands. Then she began to braid. Wow, I hadn't known you could do that! She explained that this was challah, a Jewish bread. The recipe had come from the mother of one my brother's friends. I didn't know his family was Jewish, I said. She shrugged.

In hindsight, I realize that she was always open to diverse people and foods. She descended from mostly German and English immigrants who were shaped by life in the Appalachian coal town of Johnstown in western Pennsylvania—a mostly homogenous community. She married a dashing Italian young man, my dad, a daring move at the time. When the couple settled in Northern Virginia, my mom embraced the region's international mix. Among her friends were Koreans, African Americans, Puerto Ricans, and Jews. And she always gathered new recipes to add to our basic fare of hot dogs, beef with gravy, and spaghetti— shish kebobs, fried rice, tacos, chicken with cashews, and that challah.

After she braided the two loaves of challah dough, she brushed them with an egg yolk beaten with some water. Then she handed me a small shaker bottle of poppy seeds so that I could sprinkle the loaves with tiny black dots. I watched as the seeds stuck to the glistening loaf and a few strays fell to the bottom of the baking sheet. My mom covered the loaves again for a short rise before putting them in the hot oven, where they started to puff and brown.

When the timer buzzed, she lifted her first golden brown challah loaves from the oven. A few minutes later, little poppy seeds fell to the counter as she sliced the bread. The steam warmed my hand as I took my piece. One bite won me over for good. Challah became "our" bread, the one my mom made, the one she taught me to make.

At the time, though, I knew little about Judaism and Jewish life, to which this bread turns out to be central. But in the subsequent years, every now and then, a little seed of understanding would land. Like on a sunny late spring afternoon, helping Gram, my mom's mother, plant flowers on family graves. On our way out, she drove through the hillside cemetery lined with old trees. She noted the "Jewish section" off to the side as we passed it, and I saw such names as Goldberg and Bernstein. Why a separate section, I wondered aloud? She couldn't explain the cemetery, but offered that she knew Jewish people were considered separate for not eating pork. She chuckled a bit recalling her Jewish neighbor who liked to stop by for coffee and to sneak a few slices of Gram's crispy bacon.

Or one evening, my parents, my brother, and I sat around the dining room table, eating grilled steak and a tomato and cucumber salad and watching the news on a little black-and-white TV. During a story on Israel, my dad noted with respect, "They better not mess with the Israelis." His comment caught my attention because he didn't bestow such admiration easily. He talked about how, even outnumbered, Jewish forces have repeatedly repelled legions of Arab armies using smarts and skill. I looked back to the TV to watch fighter jets taking flight across the desert, much more curious about Israel and its people.

But the biggest seed may have been that very first challah bread. When I fell in love with it that day, I had no idea what an evolving—and lasting—relationship challah and I would have.

2 large butternut squash, peeled and cubed (with inner membranes discarded and seeds reserved for toasting—see next recipe), about 7 cups

2½ cups halved or quartered shallots

2 tablespoons light brown sugar

3 large cloves of garlic, with paper skin on

1½ teaspoons kosher salt

Freshly ground black pepper

Extra-virgin olive oil

2 teaspoons minced or finely grated ginger

4 cups vegetable broth (see variation)

½ cup heavy cream

¾ cup grated fontina cheese

Roasted Butternut Squash Soup

Butternut squash, like pumpkin, was an ingredient favored by Italy's Jews. And no wonder. Fall comes and I look forward to using the buttery fruit in ravioli, tarts, and this soup. Here I roast the squash with shallots, garlic, and just a touch of brown sugar, and add fresh ginger with the broth. This soup, which has become one of my favorites, works well made a day ahead. Garnish with toasted squash seeds.

Preheat the oven to 450 degrees. Line one large baking pan or two smaller pans with aluminum foil and set aside.

Combine the squash, shallots, sugar, garlic, salt, and pepper to taste. Stir in olive oil to lightly coat. Transfer to prepared pan(s). Roast, stirring occasionally, for 30 to 40 minutes until squash is lightly browned and tender. Remove pan from oven and discard the skin from the garlic.

In a large pot, heat a layer of olive oil over medium heat. Add the ginger and sauté for 1 minute. Add 3½ cups of the broth and reserved vegetables and any juices. Simmer for 10 minutes. Purée in batches. If too thick, add broth or water until desired consistency. (At this point, soup can be refrigerated until ready to serve.)

Heat soup until bubbly and warmed through, and stir in cream in small amounts until desired taste and consistency. Add salt and pepper if needed. Garnish individual servings with fontina cheese and toasted squash seeds.

Yield: Approximately 6 cups of soup (Dairy)

Variation: You can substitute chicken broth for the vegetable broth; if keeping kosher, omit the heavy cream and fontina cheese.

Toasted Squash Seeds

So simple. So delicious. So nutritious. Toasted squash and pumpkin seeds are a fall treat I've loved since childhood. I'm happy just to snack on them, but they also add wonderful nutty flavor and crunch to soups, salads, and pastas.

Preheat oven to 375 degrees. Line a baking sheet with foil. Toss the seeds with olive oil to coat and sprinkle lightly with salt. Spread in a single layer on baking sheet. Bake 5 to 10 minutes, stirring every couple of minutes, until lightly browned. Remove and add more salt as needed. Serve hot or at room temperature.

Yield: 4 to 6 snack servings, depending on size of the squash or pumpkin (Pareve)

Seeds from one large butternut squash or medium pumpkin

Extra-virgin olive oil

Salt to taste

Meatballs
1 pound lean ground beef

$1/2$ cup finely chopped sweet onion (leftover pieces reserved)

$1/3$ cup unsalted matzah meal

$1/4$ teaspoon salt, or to taste

$1/4$ teaspoon freshly ground black pepper, or to taste

1 teaspoon dried basil

$3/4$ teaspoon garlic powder

1 large egg, lightly beaten

3 tablespoons water

Extra-virgin olive oil for frying

Matzah Batter
$1 1/4$ cups matzah meal

1 scant tablespoon salt

$1/4$ teaspoon freshly ground black pepper

Pinch of ground nutmeg

Pinch of ground red (cayenne) pepper

5 large eggs

$1/4$ cup extra-virgin olive oil

$1/4$ cup chicken broth (see note)

$1 1/2$ tablespoons chopped fresh chives

$1/4$ cup freshly opened no-sodium seltzer water

Cooking and Serving
2 quarts plus 2 cups chicken broth

Onion pieces (reserved from meatballs)

1 quart beef or chicken broth

Meatball Matzah Balls (My Jewish-Italian Dumplings)

Meatballs and matzah balls really do work together in this recipe created in honor of the book's title. These tender dumplings can be served in beef or chicken broth. But truth be told, I enjoy them just as much without the broth and instead browned and slightly crisped under the broiler (see variation); they take on a lighter texture and can be a fun appetizer this way. This recipe makes extra meatballs (so you've got something to snack on while the dumplings cook).

For the Meatballs
Mix together all the meatball ingredients except the olive oil until just combined. Heat oil in a large nonstick skillet over medium-high heat. Form meat into 1-inch balls and fry, browning well on two sides and cooking all the way through. Transfer to a paper towel–lined plate to drain and cool. Refrigerate until ready to use.

For the Matzah Batter
Whisk together the matzah meal, salt, black pepper, nutmeg, and ground red pepper. In a separate bowl, whisk the eggs until slightly frothy, then whisk in olive oil and $1/4$ cup of chicken broth. Stir in the chives. Add the wet ingredients to the dry ingredients, and stir to combine. Gently fold in the seltzer. Transfer the bowl to the freezer and chill for 30 minutes.

For the Dumplings
Cover a large plate with a piece of wax paper. Remove the matzah mixture from the freezer. Transfer a heaping tablespoon of matzah batter to wet hands. Flatten the mixture and then place a meatball in the center. Enclose the meat in the matzah batter. The ball should be a little larger than a golf ball. Place on the prepared plate and repeat with remaining matzah batter. Transfer the plate to the freezer for 15 minutes. Save leftover meatballs for another use.

Meanwhile, place the remaining chicken broth and reserved onion pieces in a large soup pot and bring to a gentle boil.

Add the meatball matzah balls to the broth, reshaping as needed.

Cover and boil gently (small bubbles regularly breaking the surface but not tossing the balls around) for 30 minutes. Meanwhile, in a separate pan, heat beef or chicken broth to be used for serving. When meatball matzah balls are done, remove with a slotted spoon. To serve, place 2 balls in each bowl with about ¼ cup of warm broth.

Yield: 18 to 20 dumplings; 9 to 10 servings each of 2 meatball matzah balls and ¼ cup of broth (Meat)

Note: You can take the ¼ cup of chicken broth for the matzah batter from the 2 quarts plus 2 cups of broth you need for cooking the balls.

Variation: To serve the meatball matzah balls on their own, preheat the broiler. Line a baking pan with nonstick aluminum foil. Arrange the cooked balls in the pan so they are not touching and broil, turning once or twice, for 15 to 20 minutes, until browned and slightly crispy.

2 large onions, cut into large pieces

5 to 6 ribs of celery, cut into large pieces

2 large carrots, peeled and cut into large pieces

2 parsnips, peeled and cut into large pieces

3 bay leaves, slightly crumpled (to release more flavor)

1 long sprig fresh rosemary

1 cup loosely packed fresh dill (a generous handful)

1 teaspoon whole black peppercorns

1/2 cup white wine, such as Pinot Grigio

4 pounds chicken parts (with bones and skin) and giblets except for liver

Cold water to cover (roughly 3 quarts)

Good Old Chicken Stock

For the best chicken soup and matzah ball soup, you've got to start with good chicken stock (that's your Jewish and Italian, and well, almost any grandmother talking). For mine, I like to use vegetables, wine, and herbs, especially dill, to bring out the best mellow chicken flavor. It's not hard at all but takes time—a great recipe to make ahead and freeze.

Place everything except the chicken and water in a very large pot (ideally a stock pot), and then add the chicken and just enough cold water to cover most of it. Slowly bring to a simmer (just small bubbles gently rising to the surface) over medium-low heat. Skim off any foam that collects on the surface. Cover loosely and simmer.

After 1 hour, remove and refrigerate any meat you want to serve in your final soup (if it cooks until the end, it will likely be dry and tough). Return any bones and scraps to the pot. Continue cooking the stock another 1 1/2 to 2 hours.

Strain the liquid through a fine-mesh strainer and discard the solids. Use right away or cool completely in the refrigerator for later use. Refrigerate for up to two days or freeze.

Yield: 2½ to 3 quarts of stock (Meat)

Tip: For especially clear broth, line the fine-mesh strainer with a double layer of cheesecloth and strain the liquid a second time.

8 cups chicken stock

¼ cup finely chopped sweet onion

¼ cup diced celery

½ cup fresh dill, chopped

Fresh egg noodles (see next recipe)

1 cup shredded cooked chicken

Kosher salt and freshly ground black pepper

Chicken Noodle Soup

Chicken noodle soup reaches its true Jewish and Italian pinnacle with homemade stock and homemade pasta noodles. These two pleasures are worth making together from scratch every now and then to enjoy just how good they can really be. The noodles come out thicker, chewier, and heartier than prepackaged dried egg noodles, and that's the way I like them. If you've made your noodles thick, they will take a little longer to cook.

Bring stock to a boil in a large pot over medium-high heat. Add onion, celery, and dill. Stir the noodles into the boiling soup a few at a time to avoid sticking. Loosely cover and reduce heat to boil gently (small bubbles regularly breaking surface) for 25 to 35 minutes or until noodles are al dente (tender, but still with some bite) or done to your liking, adding the chicken during the last 10 minutes or so. Taste and add salt and pepper as needed. Use leftovers within 2 to 3 days.

Yield: Approximately 8 cups of soup or 6 to 8 servings (Meat)

3 large eggs

1 teaspoon kosher salt

2 cups all-purpose flour, plus additional as needed

Homemade Noodles for Chicken Soup

Lightly beat the eggs and salt in a medium bowl. Gradually stir in flour to form a dense but pliable dough. If too dry, add water a teaspoon at a time; if too sticky, add just a little more flour.

Turn onto a floured surface and knead for 2 to 3 minutes until smooth. Flatten the dough to an approximate 9-inch square, lightly flour it, and wrap loosely with plastic wrap. Let the dough stand for about 30 minutes, which will make rolling easier.

Lightly sprinkle flour on a cutting board or large baking sheet lined with parchment paper, and set aside. Unwrap the dough and stretch into a rectangle with a short side toward you. Roll it with a floured rolling pin to create a large rectangle, as thin as you can get it without tearing.

Roll or fold the dough from one long side to the other. Use a serrated knife to cut ⅓-inch pieces from the roll (¼-inch pieces work well, too, if you have the patience for the cutting). Every few slices, stop, unroll the pieces and tear into desired length. Place on the prepared floured surface, being careful to keep them from touching (they'll stick if they do). When done, let noodles rest 10 minutes before adding to soup, or cover with plastic wrap and refrigerate or freeze until ready to use.

Yield: 3 to 4 cups of uncooked noodles (Pareve)

Extra-virgin olive oil

2 1/2 to 3 pounds ground turkey, beef, or chicken

Kosher salt and fresh ground black pepper

2 (14 1/2 ounce) cans diced tomatoes (fire-roasted or regular)

2 green bell peppers, cut into bite-sized pieces

2 red bell peppers, cut into bite-sized pieces

2 medium-to-large yellow or red onions, coarsely chopped

2 cans (14 or 15 ounces) dark red kidney beans, drained

1 can (15 ounces) tomato sauce (set aside 2 tablespoons in a medium bowl)

1 small can (6 ounces) tomato paste

1/4 cup of tomato ketchup

5 large garlic cloves, crushed or minced

3 tablespoons chili powder, or more to taste

1 teaspoon cumin

1/2 teaspoon dried red pepper flakes, or to taste

1/4 cup beer or water

1/3 cup plus 1 tablespoon all-purpose flour

Optional garnishes—chopped scallions and minced jalapeño peppers

Chili (Marcia's Cholent)

I could argue that my chili is both Italian and Jewish: My recipe is based on my Italian dad's version, and by ingredients and cooking method, it resembles a Jewish cholent, or Sabbath stew of beans or meat that could cook long hours. No matter how you attribute it, this robust chili gets its character from meat, onions, peppers, tomatoes, and dark red kidney beans, and it tastes even better reheated the next day. Plan for some prep time, but once everything is in the pot, you're done save for cooking some pasta to serve with it. This recipe uses a 6-quart slow cooker.

Warm a large skillet or Dutch oven over medium-high heat. If using lean meat or poultry, add a thin layer of olive oil. Break the meat or poultry into large chunks, sprinkle with salt and pepper, and brown. Transfer to a 6-quart slow cooker (leaving any rendered fat behind). Add the tomatoes, peppers, onions, beans, sauce (except for reserved 2 tablespoons), paste, ketchup, garlic, and spices to the slow cooker.

Whisk the beer or water into the reserved tomato sauce, then whisk in the flour until well blended. Fold this mixture into the chili.

Cover and cook on high setting for about 2 1/2 hours, then turn to low for about 2 hours. If cooking over a longer period, cook on high for the first hour to bring the mixture to a safe temperature before turning to low for about 8 hours.

About one hour before serving, taste and add additional spices if needed. (I often add up to one additional tablespoon of chili powder.)

Serve over warm cooked pasta and pass garnishes at the table. Leftovers freeze well.

Yield: 4 to 5 quarts (Meat)

Note: To prepare like a traditional cholent, which cooks overnight unattended after sundown on Friday, preheat the oven to 300 degrees. Prepare the ingredients but increase the amount of beer or water to 1 cup. Place in an oven-safe pan and cover tightly. Transfer to oven and turn heat to 200 degrees. Cook for about 15 hours undisturbed. If you'd like to serve with pasta, prepare the pasta before sundown, refrigerate, and toss with piping hot chili at serving time. Some pieces on the top layer of chili might blacken slightly; skim them off before serving if you like.

Matzah Balls
1¼ cups matzah meal

1 scant tablespoon salt

¼ teaspoon freshly ground black pepper

Pinch of ground nutmeg

5 large eggs

¼ cup extra-virgin olive oil

2 quarts chicken broth, divided

1½ tablespoons finely chopped fresh chives

¼ cup freshly opened no-sodium seltzer water

Soup
2 quarts homemade chicken stock

½ cup chopped fresh dill

Salt and freshly ground black pepper

Matzah Ball Soup

A few simple updates—substituting Italian olive oil for the traditional chicken fat and adding nutmeg and chives—enliven the flavor of these classic Jewish dumplings. A little seltzer gives the lighter texture that many people favor, but if you prefer matzah balls al dente like I do, simply omit the seltzer and refrigerate the balls drained. This recipe uses a lot of broth; I recommend 2 quarts of store-bought chicken broth for cooking the matzah balls and 2 quarts homemade chicken stock (see recipe on p. 12) for the soup.

For the Matzah Balls
In a medium to large bowl, whisk together the matzah meal, salt, pepper, and nutmeg. In a separate bowl, whisk the eggs until slightly frothy, then whisk in olive oil and ¼ cup of the chicken broth. Stir in the chives. Add the wet ingredients to the dry ingredients and stir to combine. Gently fold in the seltzer. Transfer the bowl to the freezer and chill for 30 minutes.

Remove the bowl. With wet hands, scoop out batter (it will be thick) and gently shape into golf ball–sized balls, about 1¼ inches in diameter. Place the shaped balls on a plate, and freeze for 15 minutes.

Warm what remains of the 2 quarts of chicken broth in a large pot over medium heat. When it just starts to boil, add the matzah balls, reshaping as needed. Cover pot and gently boil for 30 minutes, or until cooked through. The balls will expand in size as they cook.

Remove with a slotted spoon. For lightest texture, use right away. To store for later use, cover and refrigerate the matzah balls in cooled chicken broth for up to 2 days.

For the Soup
Bring to a boil 2 quarts of chicken stock along with the dill and salt and pepper to taste; boil for 10 minutes. If the matzah balls are already hot, simply ladle the warmed soup over each serving. If the balls are cooled, add them to the soup in the pot. Cook at a gentle boil (bubbles regularly breaking the surface but not tossing the contents around) until the balls are heated through, 3 to 5 minutes.

Yield: 18 to 20 matzah balls; 9 to 10 servings each of two matzah balls and ¾ cup of broth (Meat)

Variation: You can substitute an equal amount of whole-grain matzah meal for the regular matzah meal. Doing so will, as you might expect, give the dumplings a stronger and earthier grain flavor.

Extra-virgin olive oil

1 large sweet onion, chopped

2 ribs celery, coarsely chopped

2 medium zucchini, diced (about 4 cups)

Kosher salt and freshly ground black pepper

3 plum tomatoes, seeded and chopped

2 garlic cloves, pressed through a garlic press or minced

1 can (15 ounces) chickpeas, drained

1 can (15 ounces) cannellini beans, drained

8 cups vegetable broth (see variation below)

1 cup dried miniature pasta, such as mini bowties

1 package (4 or 5 ounces) fresh arugula

Freshly grated Parmesan cheese for garnish

Minestrone

Rich taste ... great texture ... excellent nutrition. This hearty Italian vegetable soup has it all. I think the fresh tomatoes and arugula along with two kinds of beans lend it especially nuanced flavor. And once you cut up the veggies, it's throw-everything-in-the pot easy.

Heat a thin layer of oil in a large pot over medium-high heat. Add the onion, celery, and zucchini and lightly season with salt and pepper. Cook, stirring frequently, 4 to 5 minutes, until the vegetables begin to soften. Add the tomatoes and garlic (and additional oil if needed) and sauté 1 minute. Stir in the chickpeas and cannellini beans. Add the broth and bring to a simmer.

Cook 10 to 15 minutes. Add the pasta and cook for the time indicated on the package. During the last minute of cooking, stir in the arugula and cook until pasta is done.

Taste and add salt and pepper if needed. Remove from heat. Ladle into bowls and sprinkle each serving with Parmesan.

Yield: About 8 servings (10 to 12 cups of soup) (Dairy)

Note: If you plan to save leftovers, cook the pasta separately and add it to each serving in the bowls. Refrigerating the leftover soup and the pasta separately will keep the pasta from getting soggy.

Variation: You can use chicken broth instead of vegetable broth; if keeping kosher, omit the cheese garnish.

Extra-virgin olive oil

1 pound kosher Polish beef sausage or turkey kielbasa, sliced into 1/2- to 3/4-inch pieces

1 large sweet onion, finely chopped

3/4 cup finely chopped celery

Kosher salt and freshly ground black pepper

2 pounds of packaged sauerkraut, drained

2 cups white wine, such as Pinot Grigio

1 cup chicken broth

8 kosher beef hot dogs

8 hot dog buns, warmed

Mashed potatoes (optional, use a nondairy version for kosher purposes; see recipe on p. 109)

Sauerkraut with White Wine and Kosher Sausage

Sauerkraut, a fermented shredded cabbage, worked its way into the cooking of both Eastern European Jews and northern Italians. But long before I knew that, I considered sauerkraut a New Year's good-luck tradition, thanks to my mother's German heritage. Her sauerkraut feast included pork, hot dogs, and mashed potatoes. My update gets flavor from kosher sausage and white wine plus onion and celery.

Heat a thin layer of oil in a large pot (ideally a Dutch oven) over medium-high heat. Add sausage and cook, turning to brown both sides, 4 to 6 minutes. Remove from pan. Add onion and celery (and more oil if needed) to the pan. Sprinkle lightly with salt and pepper. Cook, stirring frequently, until just softened, 2 to 5 minutes. Add the sauerkraut, sausage, wine, and chicken broth, and stir to combine.

Simmer partially covered for 1 hour. Increase heat slightly and gently stir in the hot dogs to submerge. Cook covered for 10 to 15 minutes, until piping hot. Remove hot dogs. The kraut mixture can be eaten on its own, on top of hot dogs, or over mashed potatoes. At the table, pass it all and let diners choose.

Yield: 6 to 8 servings (8 hot dogs, 8 to 9 cups of sauerkraut and sausage) (Meat)

Extra-virgin olive oil

4 pounds boneless beef chuck eye roast, trimmed of excess fat and cut into chunks (approximately 1½-inch pieces)

Kosher salt and freshly ground black pepper

2 medium red onions, coarsely chopped

4 medium carrots, sliced into ¼- to ⅓-inch disks

2 parsnips, peeled and sliced into ¼- to ⅓-inch disks

4 garlic cloves, crushed and coarsely chopped

⅔ cup sun-dried tomatoes, cut into strips (mix in some smoked sun-dried tomatoes if you can find them)

¼ cup (generous) all-purpose flour

2 cups red wine, such as Merlot

2 cups chicken broth

1 tablespoon Worchestershire sauce

1 tablespoon tomato paste

2 bay leaves, slightly crumpled

2 medium sprigs rosemary

Cooked egg noodles (optional)

Roasted potatoes (optional, see next recipe)

Jewish-Italian Beef Stew (Hammin)

My beef-soup-making has come a long way since my first recipe at age 8. One of my grownup variations resembles Hammin (pronounced HAH-meen), an Italian slow-cooked meat stew of Jewish origin. It uses beef chuck roast (you can ask your butcher to cut it into pieces for you) and gets incredible flavor from smoked or regular sun-dried tomatoes. I like using potatoes but prefer them crispy, so I roast them separately. The stew can be made ahead (except for the potatoes) and gently reheated the next day. This recipe uses a 6-quart slow cooker.

Heat a thin layer of olive oil in deep-sided heavy pan over medium-high heat. Add half the beef, season with salt and pepper, and brown well (about 10 minutes). Remove beef and set aside. Repeat with remaining beef. Return all meat to the pan and add the onions, carrots, and parsnips. Cook, stirring frequently, until onion begins to soften, 3 to 5 minutes. Add garlic and sun-dried tomatoes, and sauté 1 minute. Sprinkle flour over, and cook stirring constantly until well combined.

Slowly add wine and boil, stirring constantly, until slightly thickened, about 2 minutes. Stir in broth, Worcestershire sauce, tomato paste, bay leaves, and rosemary. Remove from heat and transfer mixture to the slow cooker. Cook on high 2 hours; turn to low and cook 1 to 2 more hours, until meat is tender but not falling apart. Before serving, remove bay leaves and rosemary stems and taste and adjust seasonings if needed.

Serve over noodles and, if desired, topped with roasted potatoes.

Yield: About 3 quarts of stew or 6 to 8 servings (Meat)

Roasted Potatoes
for Beef Stew

Roasting potatoes gives them that irresistible combo—tender interior and crispy exterior, all with fresh potato flavor. I think the accents of a little rosemary and paprika work additional wonders. Beyond accompanying beef stew, crispy seasoned potatoes are almost always a welcome side dish. The baking time varies depending on the potatoes' size and your desired degree of doneness.

Preheat oven to 450 degrees. Place the potatoes in a low-sided metal baking pan (preferably a jelly-roll pan). Toss potatoes with oil to thoroughly coat and stir in rosemary, salt, and pepper. Spread potatoes in a single layer, sprinkle with paprika, and bake, stirring occasionally, until tender inside and desired degree of crispiness outside, 35 to 50 minutes. Serve hot.

Yield: 4 to 5 cups (Pareve)

4 large russet potatoes, peeled and cut into 1- to 1^1/$_2$-inch pieces

Extra-virgin olive oil

2 teaspoons chopped fresh rosemary

Kosher salt and freshly ground black pepper

^{1}/$_8$ **teaspoon paprika, or more to taste**

Chapter 2

WE'VE SEARCHED THE WORLD TO GATHER THE MOST EXOTIC, PREMIUM HERBS AND SPICES SO YOU CAN CREATE AN AUTHENTIC FLAVOR ADVENTURE ALL YOUR OWN.
SALT
KOSHER FOR PASSOVER
NET WT 48 OZ (3 LB) 1.36 kg

Pasta and Grains

Whenever I can't decide what to make for dinner, I turn to pasta or rice. When I'm entertaining, the default is lasagna. When it's just my husband and me, the go-to is Mediterranean-style risotto. I never tire of these. Many of the recipes here skew Italian, though several touch on Jewish cuisine. Ravioli resembles Jewish kreplach, and this chapter's squash ravioli was inspired by Jewish-Italian recipes for ravioli with pumpkin. Jewish noodle kugels have always seemed to me like pasta dishes wanting to break out of their baking pans, so I set one free with my Italian frittata-style version featuring red peppers.

Reflections
IN THE SAUCE

Recipes
BERNEY'S ITALIAN TOMATO SAUCE

LEMON PASTA WITH CAULIFLOWER AND PEAS

LASAGNA

LESS JEWISH-GUILT LASAGNA

RISOTTO WITH SWEET ONIONS AND FETA

CHEESY BAKED PASTA WITH SPINACH AND PINE NUTS

RICE AND CHEESE BALLS

BUTTERNUT SQUASH RAVIOLI WITH SAGE BUTTER SAUCE

PASTA SALAD WITH GREEN PEAS AND SALMON

BASIL PESTO

GNOCCHI WITH VODKA SAUCE

FRITTATA KUGEL WITH ROASTED RED PEPPERS

POLENTA WITH BALSAMIC ONIONS

WALNUT POLENTA PANCAKES

In the Sauce

"NYOH-kee," she said. "No-kee," I repeated. "No," Michele said firmly, leaning closer as if that would help and using her partially closed hand to punctuate the syllables. "NYOH-keeeeee." She dragged out the word, trying to coax the right pronunciation. With my third try, we nodded in agreement that it was close enough, at least for now.

I lowered my eyes to the menu, pretending to read the rest of the choices. But I stared at the red-checked tablecloth and fiddled with the shaker of crushed red pepper flakes in the little Italian restaurant, musing over how I didn't know how to pronounce gnocchi. I didn't even know what it was.

My family wasn't that Italian, come to think of it. My half-Italian dad looked the part, with dark eyes and lightly olive skin and dark, almost black, tightly curly hair. But he didn't live it so much. He was two generations removed from the old country, Sicily, and he didn't speak Italian or tell stories that I remember about his Italian family. He worked hard, was dedicated to his family, and made some great food. We were simply an American family who ate spaghetti and meatballs with homemade sauce—always homemade sauce.

Sometimes I even forgot I was part Italian. You could never forget that Michele was Italian, though. She was the first person I had ever met so passionately connected to her Italian ethnicity. It seemed even more accentuated because she grew up in New York and embodied the boldness and bluntness—and accent—New Yorkers are known for.

The first time I met her, we were part of a group of dorm-mates walking to a little restaurant for pizza, our first day at college. She was talking to someone next to me, speaking so fast that I could barely understand her. I didn't know it was even possible to utter so many words at once. And I quickly learned that she was opinionated and full of emotion. The Virginia pizza was not spared a searing critique from the homesick New Yorker.

Over the next months, Michele made me laugh many times, and I came to admire all the might and spirit crammed into the tiny 5-foot frame that earned her the nickname "Pee wee" from one of our friends. She also had uncanny memory and dramatic timing. She could capture and hold the attention of an entire unruly group with her storytelling. She'd become so involved in the telling that she'd often rise from her chair to act parts of it out. If the tale didn't call for specific motions, sometimes she'd just pace to manage her energy and enthusiasm. Her eyes would grow wide when she reached a dramatic moment, and she knew how to pause to build suspense in her audience. Anytime she laughed, you couldn't help but laugh with her, even if you didn't know what was so funny.

One of her great passions was her full-blooded Italian heritage. Michele's strong ties to her family and culture emerged in the anecdotes she'd share about her Italian grandparents. She'd quote them with a perfect Italian accent and pepper in Italian words. I used to delight in all of this, feeling somehow a little more connected with Italian-American culture. Through her, it was colorful, brassy, and very different from the one I knew, and I was just starting to feel like I needed to go back and look a little more closely at my own roots.

But at that time I was mostly happy collecting a word, pronunciation, or anecdote here and there. Michele never minded explaining, and we especially liked talking about food. We didn't cook that much in college, but when she came to visit during summer break, she made baked ziti for us, showing me the steps along the way (and waving spoons or blocks of cheese in the air for emphasis as she talked). She apologized that this ziti was not her best rendition, because she hadn't had time to make her grandmother's tomato sauce—the sauce that always makes baked ziti and its sister dish, the bolder, more elaborate lasagna, taste best. Preparing the sauce required combining everything in the pot in the morning and leaving it to simmer on the stove all day. For Michele, nothing else compared to this smooth and slightly sweet sauce.

I knew exactly what she meant, because that's how I felt about my dad's sauce. He had revised his mother's version (much to her chagrin) to make it chunky and a little spicy. As long as I can remember, it coated our spaghetti, braised our meatballs, and enveloped our lasagna. No other sauce ever tasted as good. And Michele knew exactly what I meant. We both understood that each thought her family recipe was best. And we understood that holding such a belief was simply the Italian way. On this topic, we spoke the same language.

The next time we went to an Italian restaurant together, I ordered. "NYOH-kee." The waiter nodded as he scribbled, then he looked up again, and asked, "Are you two sisters?" The question caught us off guard, and we each studied the other's face, looking for the resemblance. We laughed at the apparent lack of any, at least to our eyes, and said no. But the question stuck with me, and thinking about it later, I could have said, in a way, yes, we are.

Extra-virgin olive oil

1 large sweet onion, coarsely chopped

1 red bell pepper, coarsely chopped

1/2 cup chopped fennel bulb

1 1/2 cups sliced fresh button or baby portobello mushrooms

5 garlic cloves, pressed through a garlic press or minced

1/2 teaspoon crushed red pepper flakes, or to taste

2 cans (14 1/2 ounces each) whole tomatoes with their juices

1 can (14 1/2 ounces) diced tomatoes with juices (preferably fire-roasted and no-salt added, such as Muir Glen brand)

3 cans (15 ounces each) tomato sauce

1 can (6 ounces) tomato paste

Freshly ground black pepper

1 teaspoon dried oregano, or to taste

1 tablespoon dried basil, or to taste

Kosher salt

Berney's Italian Tomato Sauce

To make a kosher (meatless) version of my dad's robust sauce for lasagna and other cheesy pasta dishes, I found that a little chopped fresh fennel adds just the right subtle heartiness so that you don't miss the meat. That being said, this sauce does make a wonderful base for meatballs (just remember that for kosher purposes, your meatball sauce cannot be used with cheese/dairy dishes).

Heat a layer of oil in a heavy large pot (preferably a Dutch oven) over medium-high heat. Add the onions, peppers, and fennel and sauté until just beginning to soften and brown, 5 to 7 minutes. Add the mushrooms, and sauté until tender, 2 to 4 more minutes. Add the garlic and red pepper flakes, and sauté for 1 more minute.

Stir in the whole tomatoes and use kitchen shears or the back of a spoon to break them apart slightly. Add the diced tomatoes, sauce, and tomato paste. Over medium heat, bring the mixture to a simmer. Stir in the black pepper, oregano, and basil.

Cover and simmer for 1 1/2 to 2 hours. When nearly done, taste for salt and add if needed.

Yield: 10 to 11 cups of sauce (Pareve)

4 tablespoons (1/2 stick) unsalted butter

1/3 cup fresh lemon juice (juice from about 2 large lemons)

1 1/4 cups heavy cream

1/4 teaspoon lemon extract

1/4 teaspoon orange extract

1/2 teaspoon kosher salt

1 1/2 plus 1/2 tablespoon (generous) lemon zest

1 cup plus 3/4 cup freshly grated Parmesan cheese

1 head cauliflower, washed and cut into bite-size florets

1 pound uncooked pasta shells (conchiglie)

1 package (16 ounces) frozen peas

Extra-virgin olive oil

Freshly ground black pepper

Lemon Pasta with Cauliflower and Peas

Although my take on lemon pasta is creamy, what really stands out is the light, fresh citrus flavor complemented by fruity good-quality olive oil and salty cheese. The shells and the cauliflower create a nice chewy canvas, and for contrast, the peas offer delicate bursts of flavor from inside the pasta shells, where they tend to gather. You'll need the juice and zest from about 2 large lemons for this recipe.

Bring a large pot of salted water to boil.

Melt the butter in a separate medium saucepan. Add the lemon juice, cream, lemon and orange extracts, and salt. Simmer for about 5 minutes. Remove from heat, stir in 1 cup of Parmesan cheese and 1 1/2 tablespoons lemon zest, and cover.

Meanwhile, add the cauliflower to the boiling water. Cook for 5 to 7 minutes until crisp tender and use a slotted spoon to transfer to a strainer. Add the pasta to the boiling water and cook according to package directions. During the last 5 minutes of cooking, stir in the peas. Drain the pasta and peas.

Return pasta, peas, and cauliflower to the pot. Over low heat, gently stir in the lemon sauce until mixture is just coated (if you have extra sauce, save it to use with leftovers).

Serve in individual bowls. Drizzle each serving with olive oil and sprinkle with lemon zest, grated Parmesan cheese, and freshly ground black pepper.

Yield: 6 to 8 servings (about 17 cups total) (Dairy)

1¹/₂ boxes (1¹/₂ pounds) dry lasagna noodles

2 large eggs, lightly beaten

2 pounds ricotta cheese

Freshly ground black pepper

1 recipe Berney's Italian Tomato Sauce (see recipe on p. 26)

1 pound part-skim mozzarella cheese, sliced and torn into chunks

1 cup freshly grated Parmesan cheese, plus additional for passing at the table

Lasagna

Here's my family's favored lasagna, the classic with layers of pasta, tomato sauce, and ricotta and mozzarella cheeses. Some recipes call for making a béchamel (a white sauce made with flour and milk), but this one lets the ricotta and eggs do the creamy work. Using a flavorful tomato sauce is key; I use generous helpings of my dad's thick, spicy version. You can make this ahead and plan on it feeding and pleasing a crowd.

Preheat oven to 375 degrees.

Cook noodles according to package directions until just al dente. Drain and rinse with cold water.

In a medium bowl, combine the eggs, ricotta, and black pepper.

To assemble the lasagna, spread a thin layer of sauce (approximately ¹/₂ cup) on the bottom of a large glass rectangular baking dish (preferably 15-by-10-by-2 inches). Add a single layer of noodles, cutting to fit as needed. Top noodles with spoonfuls of the ricotta mixture, spreading it to loosely cover. Dot the ricotta with mozzarella chunks. Spoon a thick ribbon of sauce over the cheeses.

Repeat, alternating the direction of the noodles with each layer, until the layers reach the top of the pan. For the final layer, cover the cheese and noodles completely with a layer of sauce. Cover tightly with foil.

Bake 25–30 minutes until bubbly and the center is hot, then uncover and sprinkle with Parmesan cheese. Bake 3–5 more minutes until cheese melts (and center of casserole reads 160 degrees on an instant-read thermometer). Remove from the oven and let rest for about 10 minutes before serving. Pass additional grated Parmesan at the table. Leftovers keep well for a couple of days in the fridge or can be frozen.

Yield: About 12 servings (Dairy)

Note: To ensure the eggs are safely cooked, the center of the lasagna must reach 160 degrees on an instant-read thermometer. If you have refrigerated the assembled casserole before cooking, plan for longer baking time.

1½ boxes (1½ pounds) dry whole-wheat lasagna noodles

⅓ cup plus 1 tablespoon egg whites or egg substitute

2 pounds low- or reduced-fat ricotta cheese (not fat free)

Freshly ground black pepper

1 recipe Berney's Italian Tomato Sauce (see recipe on p. 26)

½ pound part-skim mozzarella cheese, sliced and torn into chunks

½ pound reduced-fat mozzarella cheese, sliced and torn into chunks

1 cup freshly grated Parmesan cheese, plus additional for passing at the table

Less Jewish-Guilt Lasagna

You can make a slightly less sinful lasagna using whole wheat pasta and reduced-fat ricotta and mozzarella. There is very little difference in taste and texture (although the dominance of the wheat flavor varies across pasta brands). I served this version at a dinner party, and no one noticed the substitutions.

Preheat oven to 375 degrees.

Cook noodles according to package directions to al dente. Drain and rinse with cold water.

In a medium bowl, combine the egg whites or egg substitute, ricotta, and black pepper.

To assemble the lasagna, spread a thin layer of sauce (approximately ½ cup) on the bottom of a large glass baking dish (preferably 15-by-10-by-2 inches). Add a single layer of noodles, cutting to fit as needed. Top noodles with spoonfuls of the ricotta mixture, spreading it to loosely cover. Alternate chunks of the two different mozzarellas every couple of inches on top of the ricotta. Spoon a thick ribbon of sauce over the cheeses.

Repeat, alternating the direction of the noodles with each layer, until the layers reach the top of the pan. For the final layer, cover the cheeses and noodles completely with a layer of sauce. Cover tightly with foil.

Bake 25–30 minutes until bubbly and the center is hot, then uncover and sprinkle with Parmesan cheese. Bake 3–5 more minutes until cheese melts (and center of casserole reads 160 degrees on an instant-read thermometer). Remove from the oven and let rest for about 10 minutes before serving. Serve with additional grated Parmesan.

Yield: About 12 servings (Dairy)

Risotto with Sweet Onions and Feta

4 cups (32 ounces) vegetable broth (see note)

Extra-virgin olive oil

2 cups chopped sweet onion

Kosher salt

2 large garlic cloves, peeled and pressed through a garlic press or minced

1½ cups Arborio (short-grained) rice

½ cup (generous) light-bodied white wine, like Pinot Grigio or Sauvignon Blanc

⅓ cup plus ⅓ cup crumbled feta cheese

¼ cup (generous) freshly grated Parmesan cheese, plus additional for passing at the table

Freshly ground black pepper

One of the many things I love about creamy Italian risotto is all the possible variations. Topping the list is this pan-Mediterranean version featuring a bounty of sweet onions and the tang of feta cheese (associated with both Greek and Israeli cuisine). This recipe is inspired by one from Cooking Light *(June 1995).*

Heat broth to steaming but not boiling in a medium-sized pan over medium heat.

Meanwhile, heat a thin layer of olive oil in a medium saucepan over medium heat. Add the onion, season lightly with kosher salt, and cook stirring constantly 3 to 5 minutes, until just softened. Add garlic and cook stirring constantly for 1 more minute. Add rice (and additional oil if mixture seems dry) and stir to coat. Continue stirring for 1 to 2 minutes until the rice begins to turn translucent on the edges. Add wine, stirring until liquid is almost absorbed.

Keeping the rice mixture at a simmer, stir in ½ cup of broth, stirring every minute or so, until the liquid is almost all absorbed. Repeat with remaining liquid, but test rice for doneness before adding the last ½ cup of broth. (When done, the rice will be tender with resistance in the middle, and the mixture will be creamy.) Add the remaining broth if needed. If more liquid is needed, add a little warm water.

Remove from heat. Stir in ⅓ cup of feta cheese and the Parmesan cheese. Spoon risotto into individual bowls, and sprinkle with freshly ground black pepper and remaining feta. Serve immediately, passing additional Parmesan cheese at the table.

Yield: 4 to 5 servings (Dairy)

Note: You may substitute chicken broth for the vegetable broth if not observing kosher rules.

½ tablespoon unsalted butter

Extra-virgin olive oil

2 bunches scallions, sliced with some green parts

1 bag (10 ounces) prewashed baby spinach or 1 package (10 ounces) frozen chopped spinach, thawed and drained

4½ cups shredded sharp Cheddar cheese

2½ cups (about ⅔ pound) shredded fontina cheese

⅛ (generous) teaspoon ground red (cayenne) pepper

⅛ teaspoon ground nutmeg

¼ teaspoon kosher salt, or to taste

1 pound dry fusilli (corkscrew) pasta, undercooked by about 1 minute, drained, and rinsed under cold water

½ cup fromage blanc (preferably zero percent fat, such as Vermont Butter and Cheese brand) or reduced-fat sour cream

⅔ cup milk, preferably 2 percent

¼ cup pine nuts

Cheesy Baked Pasta with Spinach and Pine Nuts

I created this dressed-up mac 'n' lots of cheese dish for when I wanted to serve something homey but also a little more sophisticated. Spinach and scallions add depth to the cheesiness, and fat free fromage blanc contributes creamy texture without fat. Contrasting flavor and crunch comes from the pine nuts on top.

Preheat oven to 375 degrees. Butter a large 2½-liter (about 2 quarts) round casserole dish or similar-sized dish.

Warm a thin layer of olive oil in a large nonstick skillet over medium-high heat. Add the scallions and cook, stirring frequently, for 1 to 3 minutes or until just beginning to brown. Add the spinach and turn with a spatula until spinach wilts (or if using frozen spinach, until it is warmed through), 1 to 3 minutes. Remove from heat and let cool slightly.

Combine the Cheddar and fontina cheeses in a large bowl, and set aside 2½ cups for the topping. To the large bowl of cheese, add the ground red pepper, nutmeg, and salt and combine well.

Add the spinach mixture, pasta, and fromage blanc to the spiced cheese mixture. Stir gently to combine well. Transfer mixture to prepared baking dish and pour the milk over top. Top with reserved cheese. Bake for about 35 minutes, until cheese topping just starts to brown. Sprinkle with the pine nuts and bake (checking every minute or two) until the nuts are lightly browned. Serve hot.

Yield: 6 to 8 servings (Dairy)

Rice and Cheese Balls

Tender Arborio rice enclosing a chunk of fresh mozzarella, then breaded and fried—it sounds like something I'd dream up, but it's an existing delicacy. Called suppli al telefono *in Rome or* arancine *(ah-rahn-CHEE-neh) in Sicily, the traditional Italian versions often contain meat. My kosher version skips meat but adds Cheddar cheese for extra flavor and panko crumbs for a light crunch. Use a deep-fry or candy thermometer to monitor oil temperature while frying. These balls are best served hot out of the pan, but can be kept warm in a 250-degree oven.*

1 tablespoon extra-virgin olive oil

1 tablespoon unsalted butter

½ cup finely chopped onion

2 cups Arborio (short-grained) rice

1½ teaspoons salt

Freshly ground black pepper

⅛ teaspoon ground red (cayenne) pepper

½ cup freshly grated Parmesan cheese

¼ cup shredded sharp Cheddar cheese

6 ounces fresh mozzarella cheese, cut into small pieces (about the size of a large olive or blackberry)

1½ cups Japanese panko crumbs or other bread crumbs

Canola or other neutral oil (about 2 quarts, or enough to cover the balls)

Warm the olive oil and butter in a medium saucepan over medium-high heat. Add the onion and rice and cook, stirring frequently, for 1 to 3 minutes, until edges of rice turn slightly translucent and liquid is absorbed. Stir in salt, black pepper, red pepper, and 4 cups of water. Bring to boil, reduce heat to low, cover, and cook without stirring for 15 to 20 minutes, until rice is al dente and most liquid is absorbed (the mixture will be creamy). Remove from heat and stir in the Parmesan and Cheddar cheeses. Taste and add salt and pepper if needed. Set aside until cool enough to handle comfortably, about 45 minutes, or refrigerate until ready to use.

Moisten hands with water. Form about 2½ tablespoons of the cooked rice into a ball, then press 1 piece of mozzarella into the center. Reshape so that rice completely encloses the cheese, and squeeze to make a compact ball. Set aside and repeat with remaining rice. Roll the balls in the panko crumbs. If using the oven to keep cooked balls warm, preheat it to 250 degrees. Place an ovenproof baking rack over a baking sheet and set aside.

Heat oil in a heavy-bottomed, deep-sided pan (such as a Dutch oven) to 355 to 360 degrees. Working in batches of 4 to 5 balls at a time so as not to crowd the pan, gently lower the balls into the oil (be careful of splatters) and fry until deep golden brown, 3 to 4 minutes. Drain on paper towels and serve hot, or place on the prepared baking sheet and keep warm in the oven until ready to serve.

Yield: 20 to 22 balls (about 2 inches in diameter) (Dairy)

1 large butternut squash, peeled and cubed with inner membranes removed and discarded (and seeds saved for toasting if you like—see recipe p. 9) or about 1 to 1¼ pounds pre-cut butternut squash (about 5 cups)

10 shallots, peeled and quartered (about 1¼ cups)

1 tablespoon light brown sugar

1½ teaspoons kosher salt

½ teaspoon freshly ground black pepper

Extra-virgin olive oil

1 cup finely shredded Parmesan cheese, plus additional for passing at the table

Pasta

4 cups all-purpose flour, plus more as needed

1½ teaspoons salt

6 large eggs

Sauce

8 tablespoons (1 stick) unsalted butter

¼ teaspoon salt, or to taste

1½ tablespoons fresh sage, snipped into thin slivers

Butternut Squash Ravioli with Sage Butter Sauce

After I began making this ravioli, no others have ever tasted quite as good. The filling of Parmesan and roasted squash meets its match in a sauce of butter scented with sage, a native herb of the Mediterranean. Though it is a bit of work, homemade pasta gives you flavor and texture beyond compare. You can assemble the ravioli ahead and freeze (to cook, add the frozen pasta directly to the boiling water). Inspired by Joyce Goldstein's recipe for Pumpkin-Filled Ravioli—a specialty from a region in Italy once home to a thriving Jewish community—in Cucina Ebraica.

For the Filling
Preheat oven to 475 degrees.

Combine the squash, shallots, sugar, salt, and pepper in a large bowl. Stir in enough olive oil to lightly coat. Spread mixture in a single layer on one large or two smaller baking pans. Bake, stirring occasionally, for about 20 minutes or until squash is tender.

Remove and cool slightly. Lightly mash. The mixture should be cohesive but still lumpy with shallot pieces. Sir in the cup of Parmesan cheese. At this point, the filling can be refrigerated for a day.

For the Pasta
Combine the flour and salt in a large bowl. Make a well in the center of the flour and add one egg at a time, stirring in a little more flour with each addition. Combine into a ball and transfer to a lightly floured surface. Knead 1 to 3 minutes until smooth. If dough seems too dry, add water a few drops at a time; if too sticky, add flour a little at a time.

Divide the dough into five pieces and wrap each in plastic. Line a large baking sheet with parchment paper, and start heating a large pot of salted water.

Unwrap and transfer one piece of dough to a floured surface and roll it to about ⅛-inch thick or thinner if you can. Use a cookie cutter or drinking glass approximately 3 inches in diameter to cut circles in the dough. If the circles shrink after cutting, gently roll over them with the rolling pin.

Brush a light coat of water along the outside edge of the circle. Place a heaping teaspoon of filling just off center of the dough circle. Fold the dough over the filling to make a half circle, and press the edges very firmly to seal. Transfer to prepared baking sheet, spacing so ravioli don't touch. Repeat with remaining dough.

When the water is boiling, gently stir in the ravioli and adjust heat so that bubbles regularly break the surface but not so much that the pasta is thrashed about (or it may come apart). Cook until the pasta is al dente. The time will vary with the thickness of your ravioli, but count on 25 to 40 minutes. Remove the ravioli with a slotted spoon, let drain, and transfer to a warmed serving bowl.

Melt the butter. Stir in the salt and sage, and slightly crush the sage with the back of a fork. Pour over the pasta. Serve warm, passing additional grated Parmesan cheese at the table.

Yield: 40 to 45 ravioli (Dairy)

Note: Sometimes recipes suggest using wonton wrappers as the "pasta" for ravioli. Technically, yes, this works—but I don't recommend it. Although using wonton wrappers saves time in prepping and in cooking (they cook in about 15 minutes), the ravioli come out slippery and bland.

1 pound fresh salmon fillet (skin on)

Kosher salt

1 pound dry tri-color twist pasta

1 cup frozen peas

1 cup diced celery

2 medium carrots, shaved (about 1/2 cup)

1/4 cup chopped fresh Italian parsley (optional)

1/4 cup finely chopped scallions (about 2 small bunches) or onion

1/2 cup extra-virgin olive oil

5 tablespoons fresh lemon juice (the juice from about 2 medium lemons)

2 tablespoons white wine vinegar

3 tablespoons finely chopped fresh dill

1 teaspoon celery seeds

1/2 teaspoon kosher salt, or to taste

Freshly ground black pepper

Freshly grated Parmesan cheese for garnish (optional)

Pasta Salad with Green Peas and Salmon

Salmon and fresh dill are typical Jewish flavors that, combined with celery and peas, also create an easy and cool pasta salad. My mom made this recipe for years and in college I'd make it and eat it for breakfast, lunch, dinner, and sometimes just standing at the fridge door with a fork.

Place the salmon fillet flat in a saucepan, and fill pan with cool water to cover. Add 1/2 tablespoon kosher salt and bring to a boil. Turn off heat, cover, and let stand for 8 to 12 minutes, until salmon is cooked all the way through. Remove and drain. Remove and discard skin, and refrigerate salmon.

Cook the pasta according to the package directions. During the last 6 minutes of cooking, add the peas. When both are tender, remove, drain, and rinse under cool water.

In a large bowl, combine the pasta and peas, celery, carrots, parsley (if using), and scallions. In a separate small bowl, whisk together the oil, lemon juice, vinegar, dill, celery seeds, 1/2 teaspoon kosher salt (or to taste), and pepper to taste. Pour half the dressing over the pasta mixture and toss well. Add additional dressing to just coat, and reserve leftover dressing. When the salmon is well chilled, break it into chunks and gently fold it into the pasta salad. Cover and refrigerate for at least 2 hours or overnight.

Before serving, use a large spoon or spatula to gently toss the salad. Taste and add additional salt, pepper, or dressing if needed. Garnish with freshly grated Parmesan if desired.

Yield: About 14 cups of pasta salad (Pareve without cheese garnish; Dairy with cheese)

Basil Pesto

There are lots of variations on pesto (which means "pounded"), and although I enjoy them, none for me surpasses the straight-up classic basil version simply tossed with any warm pasta. The only thing I do differently is toast the garlic to tone down its pungency and let the basil flavor shine. For kosher purposes, omit the cheese if you'd like to serve the pesto with meat.

Combine basil, garlic, nuts, salt, and about half the oil in a blender or food processor. Pulse, scrapping down sides and adding oil as needed to achieve a smooth consistency. Cover tightly and refrigerate or freeze until ready to use. Stir in cheese by hand just before using. If too thick, thin with hot water until desired consistency.

Yield: About ¾ to 1 cup (without the cheese) (Dairy with cheese; Pareve without cheese)

Note: Stored pesto tends to brown quickly; to reduce this, gently pour a thin layer of olive oil to cover the top before refrigerating. You can either pour this off or stir it in before using the pesto.

3 cups loosely packed fresh basil leaves, rinsed and lightly dried

1 small garlic clove, toasted in a skillet until lightly browned and softened and then the paper skin removed

3 tablespoons pine nuts, toasted in a skillet until lightly browned

$\frac{1}{2}$ teaspoon kosher salt, or to taste

$\frac{1}{2}$ cup extra-virgin olive oil (approximate)

$\frac{1}{2}$ cup freshly grated Parmesan cheese (optional)

Gnocchi
2 pounds Yukon gold or butter potatoes

$^3/_4$ teaspoon salt

Freshly ground black pepper

2 cups all-purpose flour, plus more as needed

Vodka sauce (recipe below) or other sauce of choice

Freshly grated Parmesan cheese for garnish

$^1/_2$ cup finely chopped roasted red pepper for garnish (optional)

Vodka Sauce
Extra-virgin olive oil

2 garlic cloves, pressed through a garlic press

$^1/_8$ teaspoon crushed red pepper flakes

$^1/_8$ teaspoon dried oregano

1 can (28-ounces) crushed tomatoes

$^1/_2$ cup vodka

$^1/_2$ cup heavy cream, room temperature

$^1/_2$ cup freshly grated Parmesan cheese

$^1/_3$ cup loosely packed fresh basil leaves, chopped

Salt and freshly ground black pepper

Sugar

Gnocchi with Vodka Sauce

Italian gnocchi—dense potato dumplings—remind me a little of pierogi, the larger Polish dumplings often filled with potatoes and adopted by Eastern European Jews. No matter how you think of them, they are a pleasure, especially with a creamy kicky vodka sauce. Taste the sauce before you toss it with the gnocchi; if bitter, add sugar a pinch at a time until the flavor mellows. Chopped roasted red pepper scattered over each serving makes a flavorful garnish but it's optional. Gnocchi can be made in advance and frozen, and later boiled straight from the freezer.

For the Gnocchi
Wash potatoes and cut into large pieces. Boil until just tender. Drain. When cool enough to handle, peel and discard skin. Press potatoes through a potato ricer or mash them into a large bowl. Stir in the salt and freshly ground black pepper.

Line a baking sheet with parchment paper and set aside.

Gently fold the flour into the potatoes and knead lightly a few times to form a smooth dough that is still slightly sticky, adding more flour if too moist or sprinkling with water if too dry.

If you are cooking the gnocchi right away, bring a large pot of salted water to a boil while you shape the dumplings and start the vodka sauce (see the recipe and note on the next page).

Take a small handful of dough and roll into a rope about $^1/_2$-inch thick. Slice the rope into $^3/_4$-inch pieces. Gently pinch each piece between your finger and the prongs of a fork to give the gnocchi their characteristic ribbed texture. (If your first pieces are too sticky to shape, then add a little more flour to the dough.) Set aside on the prepared parchment. Repeat until all the dough has been shaped. If not cooking immediately, cover and refrigerate. Gnocchi can also be frozen at this point.

Place a few ladlefuls of the sauce in a large bowl and set aside. Gently stir about one-third of the gnocchi into the boiling water. After a minute or two, the dumplings will rise to the surface. Cook 40 seconds more, taste for doneness (the dumplings should be al dente), and remove quickly with a slotted spoon or a small strainer to the bowl with sauce, stirring gently to coat. Repeat with remaining gnocchi. Toss with more sauce to coat well. Serve hot with grated cheese and a scattering of chopped roasted red pepper if using.

Yield: 4 to 5 dinner servings (Dairy with cheese garnish and vodka sauce)

For the Vodka Sauce

Heat a thin layer of olive oil in a medium saucepan over medium heat. Add the garlic and red pepper flakes and sauté about 30 seconds, until garlic is fragrant and just starting to brown. Stir in oregano, tomatoes, and vodka. Simmer about 20 minutes. Stir in cream, cheese, and basil and heat through, about 5 minutes. Taste and add salt and pepper, and, if bitter, sugar (a pinch at a time) as needed.

Yield: 4 cups sauce (Dairy)

Note: To coordinate cooking the sauce with the gnocchi, prepare the sauce through the 20-minute simmer. Remove from heat and set aside until almost ready to boil gnocchi, then re-warm sauce and proceed with the recipe.

½ box (8 ounces) dry uncooked spaghetti

4 large eggs

1 cup jarred roasted red peppers, drained, blotted dry, and puréed

¾ cup plus ¼ cup freshly shredded part-skim mozzarella cheese

¾ cup plus ¼ cup freshly grated Parmesan cheese

½ teaspoon (generous) salt, or to taste

½ teaspoon (scant) freshly ground black pepper, or to taste

2 scallions (white and some green parts) finely chopped

Dash of ground red (cayenne) pepper

½ tablespoon unsalted butter

½ tablespoon extra-virgin olive oil

Frittata Kugel with Roasted Red Peppers

Here I nudge the mild-mannered Jewish noodle kugel (baked pudding) in an Italian direction with spaghetti, roasted red peppers, and Italian cheeses plus a quick cooking method similar to that used for frittatas. This versatile, flavorful pasta "cake" can be sliced and served as a main or side dish or even an appetizer. Jarred roasted peppers work fine here.

Cook the spaghetti according to the package directions, except undercook by about 1 minute. Drain.

Lightly beat the eggs in a medium bowl. Stir in the puréed red peppers, the ¾ cup of mozzarella, the ¾ cup of Parmesan, salt, pepper, scallions, and cayenne pepper. Add the pasta and gently toss to combine well.

Preheat the broiler.

Heat the butter and oil in a medium-size oven-safe skillet (such as a 9-inch cast iron skillet) over medium-high heat. When hot, swirl to combine and add the pasta mixture. Gently press to create an even layer. Cook about 3 minutes, until the bottom is golden brown.

Transfer the skillet to the oven. Broil until the top is golden brown and the mixture is set, 5 to 7 minutes. Remove from the oven and cool slightly. Loosen the sides and invert onto a plate. Immediately sprinkle with ¼ cup of mozzarella and ¼ cup of Parmesan. Once cheeses melt, slice the pie into wedges, and serve warm or at room temperature.

Yield: 8 side-dish servings (Dairy)

Polenta with Balsamic Onions

Extra-virgin olive oil

1 large sweet onion, thinly sliced

Kosher salt and freshly ground black pepper

1 tablespoon balsamic vinegar

1 cup milk, preferably whole

2 cups water

1 cup cornmeal

1 cup frozen corn kernels, thawed

3 tablespoons unsalted butter

$^3/_4$ cup plus $^1/_4$ cup grated Asiago cheese

There's a Jewish version of polenta ("cornmeal mush") that features raw onions. I think the creamy, delicious Italian dish deserves something sweeter and softer, hence my version with browned sweet onions flavored with a splash of balsamic vinegar. I like using the slightly more assertive Asiago (rather than Parmesan) to face up to the onions and corn kernels for a boost of flavor and texture. Many recipes call for constant stirring, but if you keep the heat low, intermittent stirring works just fine.

Heat a generous layer of oil in a large nonstick skillet over medium-high heat. Add onion and season lightly with salt and pepper. Cook, stirring frequently, for 5 to 8 minutes, until the pieces soften and turn golden brown. Stir in vinegar. Remove from heat and set aside.

Combine milk with 2 cups of water in a medium saucepan and bring to a boil. Add a generous pinch (about $^1/_4$ teaspoon) kosher salt. Reduce heat to simmer. Gradually add cornmeal in a steady stream, whisking to incorporate. Stir in the corn kernels. Return to a boil, then turn heat to low (so that mixture just barely simmers).

Cook, stirring thoroughly every few minutes for about 20 minutes, until cooked through and creamy. Remove from heat. Stir in butter and $^3/_4$ cup of Asiago cheese. Add salt and pepper to taste. Transfer to a serving dish and top with $^1/_4$ cup Asiago and the cooked onions. Serve immediately.

Yield: About 4 cups, or 4 to 5 servings (Dairy)

Polenta

1 cup milk, preferably whole

2 cups water

Kosher salt

1 cup cornmeal

1 cup frozen corn kernels, thawed

3 tablespoons unsalted butter

1 cup freshly grated Parmesan cheese

Freshly ground black pepper

Olive oil, additional butter, or cooking spray for coating baking sheet and plastic wrap

Pancakes

1/2 cup freshly grated Parmesan cheese

1 teaspoon chopped fresh rosemary

1 tablespoon unsalted butter, melted

1/3 cup finely chopped walnuts

Walnut Polenta Pancakes

Cold polenta is so thick you can cut it, and that's a very good thing if you have pancakes in mind. Topped with Parmesan, rosemary, and walnuts and baked until crispy, these cakes work as a good appetizer, side dish, or garnish to a thick stew.

Combine milk with 2 cups of water in a medium saucepan and bring to a boil. Add a generous pinch (about 1/4 teaspoon) kosher salt. Reduce heat to simmer. Gradually add cornmeal in a steady stream, whisking to incorporate. Stir in the corn kernels. Return to a boil, then turn heat to low (so that mixture just barely simmers).

Cook, stirring thoroughly every few minutes for about 20 minutes, until cooked through and creamy. Remove from heat. Stir in butter and cheese. Add pepper to taste.

Butter or oil a baking sheet. Spread the polenta on the sheet to a thickness of 1/2 inch (see note). Let cool slightly, then cover with greased plastic wrap and chill until very firm, at least 4 hours or overnight.

To make the pancakes, preheat the oven to 375 degrees and lightly grease 1 larger baking sheet or 2 regular-sized baking sheets. Slice the cold polenta into approximate 2 1/2-inch squares and transfer to the prepared baking sheet(s), leaving space between pieces to allow them to spread and crisp up during baking. Brush tops with melted butter. Combine the Parmesan cheese and rosemary and sprinkle over polenta slices. Bake until just starting to brown, about 25 minutes, then sprinkle with walnuts and continue baking until edges are dark brown and crispy, about 35 more minutes.

Remove from oven and cool in the pan a few minutes. Transfer to a paper-towel lined plate and serve hot.

Yield: About 20 pancakes (Dairy)

Note: You can use greased or nonstick foil to block the hot polenta from spreading too thin on larger baking sheets; the polenta will take up about three-quarters of a standard-sized (15-by-10-inch) pan.

Chapter 3

Meat, Poultry, and Fish

These meat, poultry, and fish dishes encompass a sampling of diverse recipes, from homey (like turkey meat loaf) to dressy (salmon in parchment paper). My basics are Italian meatballs and two different recipes for Jewish beef brisket, plus my dad's recipe for grilled steak with lemon. But I've become equally attached to newer recipes developed for this collection, including chicken with Italian salsa verde and a beloved restaurant seafood recipe that I revised to make kosher and akin to a Jewish-Italian dish of baked fish and artichokes.

You might see the biggest difference between Jewish and classic Italian recipes in the kosher rules—no pork or shellfish and no dairy combined with meat. Also missing from this book is one classic Jewish ingredient—schmaltz, or rendered chicken fat (used like lard or oil). Years ago, schmaltz allowed Jewish cooks to use every possible component of poultry. I know it adds great flavor but I use healthier alternatives, usually olive oil, when a recipe calls for fat.

Reflections
THE LEMON TREE

Recipes
ITALIAN MEATBALLS

GRILLED STEAK WITH LEMON, OREGANO, AND GARLIC

TURKEY MEAT LOAF

CHICKEN WITH ITALIAN SALSA VERDE

SALMON AND VEGETABLES IN PARCHMENT PAPER

CHICKEN ROASTED WITH GARLIC AND HERBS

BAKED SEA BASS WITH ARTICHOKES, MOZZARELLA, AND OLD BAY SEASONING

BEEF BRISKET WITH CRANBERRIES AND MUSHROOMS

TANGY BEEF BRISKET

TUNA AND VEGETABLE KEBOBS

The Lemon Tree

Every few years when I was growing up, my Italian grandma came to visit for a couple of weeks. She was a tiny woman with hair dyed black, and she always carried with her suitcases with floral upholstery. I remember her arrival one summer when I was a child. We gathered around as she opened her suitcase on the dining room floor.

She gently ruffled through a few blouses and pants, and pulled out two lemons. Then she folded back some clothes from the other corner of the suitcase and pulled out a few more lemons. They were the biggest lemons I had ever seen. They were gnarly and uneven but plump and inviting and a cheerfully rich yellow.

They came from the lemon tree in Grandma's brother and sister's backyard in San Jose, California. I pictured the tree that could produce such wonders. I imagined it as tall as a single-story house, round and full with its densely green branches weighed down from so many lemons fat with pulp and juice. How nice it would be to have a lemon tree, I thought. My parents gently rebuffed my request for one, explaining that Virginia's winters would be too cold for it.

So the lemons remained for me a symbol of idealized California life—sunny and filled with nature's bounty. Healthy and brash and both sweet and tart. And a little symbolic of my grandma, though she skewed to the tart side, or so we often thought. I say that because she had a forceful personality and immovable points of view on the world. At times, it seemed worth trying to change her mind about something, but once engaged in the task, we too often wondered why we had ever started. My family learned there was no changing this circumstance, only adapting to it. One way was to keep the visits infrequent.

While she flew east every few years, we never went west to visit her in San Jose, where she had moved long before to join her parents, brothers, and sisters—all of whom had migrated from western Pennsylvania. Our infrequent contact lent me little information about the Sicilians in my bloodline.

A post-college trip with my friends Josie and Shirley combined with a sense of curiosity and adventure finally helped me find my way to San Jose. When I called a few weeks prior to tell Grandma that my friends and I were coming, her voice melted with happiness. She kept saying that she could not wait to see us and introduce us to her friends and some of the family.

When we pulled our road trip car, Josie's Volkswagen Quantum, into a spot in front of Grandma's apartment building, Grandma threw open her sixth-floor window and leaned out to wave and call to us. She also shouted instructions for exactly how to park and what to do. That was my grandma.

Her one-bedroom apartment was very tidy and pretty. Her furniture was upholstered in blue and gold. I decided blue must be her favorite of the two because she also had blue carpet, a blue centerpiece mat, and blue glass roosters in the living room. Grandma proudly showed us around, pointing out prized ceramic pieces. But she had one set of cherished possessions that she saved for family, and this was an especially momentous family occasion.

She opened a closet and pulled out boxes and envelopes of old family photos. We sat down on her bed and began to spread out the images. A large one caught my eye—a family portrait. On the left was my three-year-old dad with curly dark hair and wearing a sailor outfit. He was propped on the sofa arm, and his father's hand steadied him around the waist. My grandfather, dashingly dressed in a dark three-piece suit, had a long face and slightly bemused smile. Next to him was Grandma, a beautiful trim young woman with dark hair pinned up in tight curls around her face, wearing a dress with braids on the short sleeves. I raised another photo, one of Grandma's parents, looking very much like Italian immigrants. Her father stood proudly in a three-piece suit with a pocket watch. He had a full head of nicely combed-back short hair with white showing on the sides above his ears. Her mother, a short round woman, wore a dark polka dot dress and graying hair gathered wispily away from her face. She looked tired but happy. There were also Grandma's sisters and brothers. And my goodness, they all made a handsome family.

We stopped to eat, and after lunch, we drove to Grandma's brother and sister's home—a small white clapboard house that their parents built in the 1930s. As Jimmie and Anne opened the door for us, I thought how Italian they looked, Anne short with dark eyes, dark hair, and a round face; Jimmie short like his sisters, with a round face wrinkled all along the smile lines, and light blue eyes. They laughed generously and brimmed with excitement. At that moment, I regretted not meeting them sooner.

They wanted to hear all about my dad and mom and brother, and about our trip. I wanted to hear about their lives and their parents. I wanted to know—but did not ask—how they could be so different from Grandma. They planned to take us out for spaghetti and meatballs but first showed us around the house.

We walked out the back door into the sunlit yard. And there it was. The lemon tree. I almost didn't recognize it because it wasn't how I imagined it at all. It was shorter, narrower, and more delicate. The tree stood by the kitchen window, haggard but proud of its life's work. Like the occupants inside the house, it had Mediterranean roots—figuratively at least—because lemon trees had been cultivated in Italy for thousands of years.

Although there were few lemons at this point in the growing season, I found one and picked it. I thanked the tree for waiting all those years for me to come.

That night, after everyone else went to sleep, I stared at the ceiling thinking about what a fateful stop San Jose turned out to be. I found a pen and began writing a postcard to Daryl, a sweet and funny Jewish man I had just started dating.

2 pounds lean ground beef

³/₄ cup finely chopped sweet onion

2 thick slices of nondairy sandwich bread (with crusts discarded), thoroughly soaked in water and gently squeezed of excess

³/₄ teaspoon salt, or to taste

1¹/₂ teaspoons garlic powder

1¹/₂ teaspoons dried oregano

Freshly ground black pepper

2 large eggs

Extra-virgin olive oil

Berney's Italian Tomato Sauce (see p. 26)

Italian Meatballs

It seems like we can never have too many of these meatballs, a childhood favorite of mine. Browned in olive oil and braised in tomato sauce, the seasoned beef becomes tender and richly flavored with spices and tomatoes. Serve the meatballs as appetizers or with the cooking sauce over warm pasta. The only significant change I've made to my mom and dad's tried-and-true recipe is to omit the cheese to make them kosher (see note).

Mix beef and next seven ingredients (through eggs) together in a bowl until just combined. Heat a thin layer of olive oil in a large pan (such as a Dutch oven or frying pan) over medium-high heat.

Roll the meat mixture into balls about 1¹/₂ inches in diameter (or to desired size). Place as many as will fit in a single layer in the hot oil, and fry, turning to brown on at least two sides. Remove with a slotted spoon to a plate. Repeat with any remaining meatballs.

Assemble the sauce and when warm, stir in the meatballs. Simmer for at least 1 hour. Use a slotted spoon to remove from sauce if serving as an appetizer, or spoon meatballs and sauce over warm cooked pasta.

Yield: 30 to 40 meatballs (1½-inch diameter) (Meat)

Note: If you are not observing kosher rules, you may also add ¼ cup finely grated Parmesan cheese to the meat mixture.

½ cup fresh lemon juice
(4 to 5 lemons)

1 tablespoon dried oregano

4 garlic cloves, pressed through a
garlic press

½ teaspoon kosher salt, or to
taste

Freshly ground black pepper

4 individual serving-size rib-eye
steaks, about 1½ inches thick
(2½ to 3 pounds of meat)

Grilled Steak with Lemon, Oregano, and Garlic

A traditional Sicilian preparation of steak includes lemon and garlic—and my dad always used both and a few other spices to marinate his sirloin steaks. Since kosher sirloin steak is usually not available, I use rib-eye steaks here.

About 30 minutes before cooking, combine the lemon, oregano, garlic, salt, and pepper in a large zip-top plastic bag; in a separate bowl, reserve 2 tablespoons of marinade to brush on steaks during grilling. Add steaks to the lemon mixture and turn to coat. Marinate the steaks at room temperature, turning every 10 minutes or so for 30 minutes.

Meanwhile, coat the grill rack with cooking spray, and preheat the grill to medium-high.

Remove the steaks and discard the used marinade. Season with additional black pepper on both sides, and place on hot grill. Cover and sear each side for 2 to 3 minutes, then reduce heat slightly and grill it to desired doneness (10 to 15 minutes for medium). Brush with reserved marinade about halfway through.

Let the steaks rest a few minutes before serving.

Yield: 4 servings (Meat)

Meat Loaf

Extra-virgin olive oil

1½ cups chopped sweet onion (about 1 medium to large onion)

½ cup finely chopped celery

¾ teaspoon kosher salt

¼ teaspoon freshly ground black pepper, or to taste, plus more for topping

1 teaspoon dried basil

⅛ teaspoon crushed red pepper flakes

1 teaspoon dried oregano

1 cup finely chopped baby portobello mushrooms

4 garlic cloves, crushed and coarsely chopped

½ cup chicken broth

2 teaspoons tomato paste

1 cup panko crumbs (or 2 slices of nondairy sandwich bread, crusts discarded) (see note)

2 pounds ground turkey, preferably 1 pound ground turkey breast and 1 pound ground turkey thigh

2 large eggs, lightly beaten

Glaze

3 tablespoons chicken broth

1 tablespoon steak sauce (such as Heinz 57)

2 tablespoons light brown sugar

1 tablespoon cornstarch

Turkey Meat Loaf

Once I got this recipe right, it changed my conception of meat loaf from something ordinary to something comfortingly special. I think the garlic, celery, and mushrooms and the sweet/spicy glaze bring out the best flavors of the ground turkey and help keep the loaf moist. This home-style pleasure can be served warm or cold.

Preheat the oven to 375 degrees. Line a large jelly-roll pan or rimmed cookie sheet with heavy-duty aluminum foil and set aside.

Heat a thin layer of olive oil in a medium skillet over medium-high heat. Add the onion, celery, salt, pepper, basil, red pepper flakes, and oregano. Cook, stirring often, until the onion is softened but not browned, 5 to 8 minutes. Add the mushrooms, and cook a few more minutes until softened. Stir in the garlic and cook stirring constantly for 1 more minute. Remove from heat and set aside to cool slightly. Stir in the broth, tomato paste, and panko.

Combine the glaze ingredients in a small bowl and set aside.

Combine the turkey, eggs, and onion mixture in a large bowl. Mix well with a fork or your hands until just combined. Transfer to the prepared baking pan and shape into a rectangular loaf about 1-inch thick. Brush top and sides with glaze, and sprinkle top with freshly ground black pepper. Bake for 45 to 55 minutes, until a thermometer inserted into the middle of the loaf reads 165 degrees.

Let rest about 10 minutes before slicing into approximate 1-inch slices and serving. Also good at room temperature and cold. Leftovers freeze well.

Yield: 5 to 7 servings (2 slices per serving) (Meat)
Note: For kosher observance, the crumbs or bread must be nondairy.

Sauce

3/4 cup Italian parsley leaves

1/4 cup fresh mint leaves

1/2 cup baby spinach leaves

2 teaspoons tiny capers
(preferably nonpareil, the
smallest size), rinsed and drained

2 tablespoons toasted pine nuts

1/2 teaspoon white wine vinegar

1/2 teaspoon Dijon mustard

Freshly ground black pepper

1/4 teaspoon (scant) kosher salt

1/2 cup (scant) extra-virgin olive
oil

Chicken

4 boneless, skinless chicken
breasts, about 1 1/2 pounds total,
lightly pounded to an even
thickness of about 1/2 inch

Freshly ground black pepper

Extra-virgin olive oil

Cornmeal

Chicken with Italian Salsa Verde

Italian salsa verde, or green sauce, both looks and tastes deliciously fresh. I think this combination of fresh herbal flavors works wonders over a simple cornmeal-crusted boneless chicken breast. (But don't feel limited—it's a traditional Italian-Jewish topping for hard-boiled eggs, and it brightens mild chicken, turkey, and fish dishes.) The sauce can be made a day or two in advance and stored in the refrigerator. It's worth brining the chicken if you are not using kosher meat (see note).

Prepare the sauce by placing all the sauce ingredients except for the olive oil in a blender. Add about half the oil and pulse, processing and adding additional oil until smooth and desired consistency. Set aside.

Heat a thin layer of olive oil in a large nonstick skillet over medium-high heat. Season the chicken pieces with black pepper, turn to coat in cornmeal, and add to the pan. Cook for about 6 minutes, until bottom is golden brown, and then turn and cook until the other side is browned and chicken is cooked through, 3 to 5 more minutes. If chicken is browning too much before the inside is done (165 degrees on an instant-read thermometer), lower heat slightly and loosely cover the pan, checking frequently for doneness.

Remove the chicken. Serve breasts whole or sliced and topped with salsa verde.

Yield: About 4 servings of chicken (Meat); about 1/2 cup salsa verde (Pareve)

Note: If not using kosher chicken (which is already salted), boost the flavor and moisture by brining the chicken before cooking: Soak the chicken in 1 quart of cold water with 1/4 cup of dissolved kosher salt in the fridge for 1 hour. Rinse, pat dry, and proceed with the recipe.

Extra-virgin olive oil

1 large red bell pepper, seeded and sliced thin lengthwise

1 cup celery (about 3 ribs), sliced thin into 2-inch strips

1 large sweet onion, sliced into rings and then sliced and separated into 2- to 3-inch strands

Kosher salt

4 pieces salmon fillet (about 2 pounds), gently washed and patted dry

Freshly ground black pepper

Ground red (cayenne) pepper

Salmon and Vegetables in Parchment Paper

After trying salmon in parchment paper (en papillote) in a restaurant, I started experimenting. Salmon, celery, red pepper, and onion became my favorite combination; everything becomes melt-in-your-mouth tender and mildly sweet after baking in the paper packets. It's easy yet festive—I've even served it at a Passover Seder. I've described the way I cut and fold the parchment paper to hold the salmon, but feel free to improvise, and if you can't find parchment, use foil.

Preheat the oven to 475 degrees.

In a large nonstick skillet, heat a thin layer of olive oil. Add the vegetables, sprinkle lightly with salt, and sauté for approximately 6 minutes until softened and lightly browned (adding more oil if needed). Set aside.

Meanwhile, prepare the parchment paper. Tear 4 pieces of paper each about 18 inches long. Fold each piece in half, and then holding the folded side, cut a half-circle that is at least 3 inches wider than the fish.

Open the parchment circles and place each fillet, skin side down, longwise next to the crease. Brush each fillet with olive oil, then sprinkle with kosher salt and black pepper. Dust lightly with cayenne pepper.

Spoon ¼ of the vegetable mixture over each fillet (some vegetables can fall to the sides of the fish). Then fold the parchment over the fish to close the half-circle. Seal the edges with narrow folds. The paper should stay closed but does not need to be tight. To avoid leakage, crimp edges slightly upward.

Place packets on an ungreased baking sheet and bake for 20 to 25 minutes, until the parchment starts to brown. Open one packet to test fish—it should flake easily and be opaque.

Serve individual packets at the table or open the packets in the kitchen and arrange fillets and vegetables on a serving platter.

Yield: 4 servings (Pareve)

4 medium heads of garlic, cloves separated and peeled (or 2 cups of jarred cloves, rinsed and drained)

1 cup shallots, peeled and halved (or quartered if very large)

Extra-virgin olive oil

4 to 5 pounds of skin-on, bone-in chicken pieces, trimmed of excess fat, rinsed and patted dry

Freshly ground black pepper

3/4 cup dry white wine such as Pinot Grigio

1 cup chicken broth

2 sprigs fresh thyme

1 sprig fresh rosemary

1 bay leaf, slightly crumpled

2 tablespoons chopped rosemary

2 tablespoons chopped Italian parsley

2 tablespoons chopped fresh thyme

2 tablespoons cornstarch or potato starch (optional)

Chicken Roasted with Garlic and Herbs

Fresh herbs and lots of garlic elevate roasted chicken, a regular at Jewish holiday dinners. This recipe feeds a crowd. You can save time by using jarred peeled garlic cloves, but I don't think they are as flavorful or tender as fresh garlic—using half fresh and half jarred is a good compromise.

Preheat the oven to 425 degrees.

Combine the garlic, shallots, and olive oil to coat in the bottom of a large baking pan. Cover and bake for 20 to 25 minutes, stirring once about halfway through. Remove from oven.

Meanwhile, heat a thin layer of oil in a large skillet over medium-high heat. Add a single layer of chicken, and season with black pepper. Brown both sides, 10 to 12 minutes. Repeat with remaining chicken. Remove to a plate.

Add the wine, chicken broth, thyme sprigs, rosemary sprig, and bay leaf to the roasting pan. Arrange the browned chicken pieces, skin side up, on top. Combine the chopped rosemary, parsley, and thyme and sprinkle over the chicken. Cover the pan and roast for 30 to 45 minutes, or until a thermometer inserted in the thickest part of the breast and legs reads 165 degrees. For crisper skin, remove the cover and broil the chicken until browned, 2 to 6 minutes more.

Remove the pan from oven. Arrange the chicken pieces on a platter along with a handful of the cooked garlic cloves and shallot pieces. Strain the pan juices, pressing a few garlic cloves through the strainer into the liquid, and skim any visible fat.

You can serve the juices with the meat, or if you prefer gravy, bring the juices to a boil. In a small bowl, combine 2 tablespoons of potato starch or cornstarch with about 1/4 cup of water. Gradually stir the starch mixture into the boiling juices just until thickened to desired consistency.

Yield: 6 to 8 servings (Meat)

Baked Sea Bass with Artichokes, Mozzarella, and Old Bay Seasoning

1³/₄ to 2 pounds sea bass, skinned and deboned, rinsed, dried, and cut into 1- to 1¹/₂-inch-cubes (see note)

2 cans (14 ounces each) artichoke hearts packed in water, well drained and coarsely chopped

2 tablespoons unsalted butter, melted

2 tablespoons fresh lime juice (juice of about 1 lime)

¹/₈ teaspoon kosher salt, or to taste

2¹/₂ to 3 teaspoons Old Bay Seasoning, or to taste

2¹/₂ cups shredded part-skim, low-moisture mozzarella cheese

¹/₂ cup shredded provolone cheese

This is one of my favorite creations—an easy, baked fish dish that is mild, buttery, cheesy, and accented with Old Bay Seasoning (created by a German Jewish immigrant). The recipe draws inspiration from a beloved scallop-and-crab restaurant dish from my pre-Judaism days and also from the Jewish-Italian dish of mild fish baked with artichokes.

Preheat the oven to 450 degrees.

Toss the fish and artichokes with the melted butter and lime juice in a 9-by-13-inch glass baking dish. Sprinkle with kosher salt and a generous layer of Old Bay Seasoning. Bake until fish is done (it should flake easily with a fork and be opaque all the way through), 12 to 18 minutes.

Remove from oven. Turn the broiler on high. Top the fish and artichokes evenly with mozzarella and provolone. Broil the casserole until the cheese is melted and just lightly browned in spots, 3 to 5 minutes. Cool slightly before serving.

Yield: Approximately 6 servings (Dairy)
Note: If you need a substitute for sea bass, a good option is sablefish.

5 to 6 pounds beef brisket (one to two pieces of meat), trimmed of large pieces of fat

Kosher salt and freshly ground black pepper

Extra-virgin olive oil

10 garlic cloves, sliced into 3 or 4 slivers each

2 large onions, sliced

1 cup red wine, such as Merlot or Cabernet Sauvignon

2 cans (10½ ounces each) concentrated chicken broth, such as Manischewitz brand

½ cup thawed frozen cranberry juice concentrate

½ cup matzah cake meal or all-purpose flour

2 tablespoons fresh rosemary

12 to 14 ounces of cremini or baby portobello mushrooms

¾ cup dried cranberries

Beef Brisket with Cranberries and Mushrooms

There's something special about the fruitiness and earthiness that cranberry juice, wine, and mushrooms give to this tender brisket. It's become a go-to for holiday get-togethers, especially because it is best made a day ahead. Be sure to remove it from the oven as soon as the meat gets tender. This version evolved over the years from a newspaper-clipped version that we lost after the first try.

Season the brisket with salt and pepper. Heat a thin layer of olive oil in a large skillet over medium-high heat. Add the beef and brown both sides. Remove from heat.

Preheat the oven to 325 degrees.

Using a sharp knife, cut openings an inch or two apart all across the top of the meat and insert the garlic slivers. Toss any leftover garlic pieces along with the onions in the bottom of a large roasting pan. Place the brisket (garlic-side up) on top.

Whisk together the wine, chicken broth, cranberry juice, and matzah cake meal or flour in a medium bowl. Stir in rosemary. Gently pour the wine mixture over the meat; the liquid should reach no more than about halfway up the sides of the meat (the liquid will rise as the meat cooks). Cover tightly and roast just until the beef is fork tender, 4 to 5 hours.

Remove the pan from the oven. Strain the sauce through a fine-mesh strainer and discard the solids. Refrigerate meat and sauce separately overnight.

The next day, skim and discard any fat from the sauce. Slice the beef against the grain and arrange it in an ovenproof dish. Scatter the cranberries on top.

Clean and slice the mushrooms. Heat a thin layer of olive oil in a large skillet over medium-high heat. Add the mushrooms and season lightly with salt and pepper. Sauté until just beginning to brown and soften, 3 to 5 minutes, adding more oil as needed. Add 1 to 1¼ cups of the reserved sauce and cook, stirring, another 1 to 2 minutes until hot and bubbly. Remove from heat and let cool slightly. Spoon warm mushrooms and sauce over the brisket and cranberries.

Cover and refrigerate until ready to serve. (The dish can be frozen at this point; thaw partially in refrigerator before proceeding.)

To serve, reheat covered in a 350-degree oven for about 40 minutes (longer if frozen) or until heated through. Warm remaining sauce on the stove or in the microwave (see note). Pass the sauce with the meat.

Yield: 4 to 6 servings (Meat)

Note: If the sauce needs to be thickened, bring it to a boil in a medium saucepan. In a small bowl, combine 2 tablespoons of potato starch (or cornstarch if not Passover) and about ¼ cup of water. A little at a time, add the starch mixture to the boiling sauce, stirring constantly, just until the sauce reaches desired thickness.

Meat
4 to 5 pounds brisket of beef, trimmed of excess fat

Kosher salt and freshly ground black pepper

Sauce
2 large onions, diced

2 garlic cloves, minced

1 bottle (14 ounces) ketchup

1 heaping tablespoon brown sugar

1½ tablespoons Worcestershire sauce

1 tablespoon dry mustard

1 tablespoon red wine vinegar

½ teaspoon chili powder

½ teaspoon paprika

½ teaspoon salt

1¼ cups water

2 bay leaves

Tangy Beef Brisket

Our friend Victoria's mother, Maxine Rapoport—an author of many cookbooks—has been making brisket this way for years and serves it with mashed potatoes, potato latkes, or noodles. The brisket comes out tender, tangy, and slightly sweet. It can be made ahead, and leftovers make great sandwiches.

Preheat the oven to 325 degrees.

In a skillet or Dutch oven over medium-high heat, brown brisket. If meat is too large to fit in pan, cut into two pieces and brown separately. Salt and pepper to taste after browning, and transfer to a large Dutch oven or roasting pan.

In a separate bowl, stir together all the ingredients for the sauce. (To remove all the ketchup from the bottle, pour some of the water into the bottle and shake; pour into sauce mixture.) Pour the mixture over the meat.

Cover with foil and roast for 3 to 3½ hours, basting halfway through baking time. Meat is done when it can be pulled apart with a fork and is no longer pink inside.

Cool slightly before slicing. Spoon a little sauce over the meat, and save the rest of the sauce to pass at the table. If freezing meat, wrap the sliced meat in plastic and then foil before placing in the freezer. Freeze sauce separately. Reheat covered loosely with foil, with some of the sauce spooned underneath and over top of the meat, in a 325-degree oven.

Yield: 6 servings (Meat)

3/4 pound tuna steaks, cut into 1-inch cubes (see note)

1 each of green, red, and yellow bell pepper, seeded and sliced into 1 1/2-inch chunks

1 pint cherry tomatoes

2 medium red onions, cut into large chunks

1 lime, halved

Extra-virgin olive oil

Garlic powder

Kosher salt

Freshly ground black pepper

Tuna and Vegetable Kebobs

I asked my brother to make fish-based Middle Eastern–style kebobs with vegetables for a holiday dinner one year—and his rather spur-of-the-moment creation turned out to be a winner for both flavor and simplicity. The mild fish and bright peppers and tomatoes go well with just about anything, but especially with risotto or polenta for a pan-Mediterranean meal. If using wood skewers, soak them in water for 30 minutes before using.

Lightly grease the grill rack. Preheat the grill to medium-high.

Alternate tuna, peppers, tomatoes, and onions on four or five metal or wood skewers. Squeeze lime juice and drizzle olive oil over kebobs. Sprinkle with garlic powder, salt, and pepper.

Place skewers on the hot grill. Cook over medium-high heat, turning every couple of minutes, 5 to 10 minutes total, until fish is desired degree of doneness.

Yield: 4 to 5 kebobs on 12- to 14-inch skewers (Pareve)

Note: My brother originally used swordfish, which is often used in Sicilian cooking and is very good for grilled kebobs. However, some Jewish authorities do not consider swordfish kosher.

Chapter 4

Breads

Homemade bread takes some work, yes, but what an amazing payoff in flavor and texture. Hot out of the oven? Wow. Beyond that, bread offers a beautiful symbol of the hands-on generosity that both Jews and Italians value—something to give, be grateful for, share, and enjoy.

Most recipes begin with similar ingredients—flour, yeast, and water. The flavors and characteristics diverge with additions of butter or oil, sugar or herbs, or vegetables or cheese. And leftover bread lives a whole second (delicious) life—as pizzas, French toast, and crisps. This chapter's recipes range from Jewish bialys and challah to Italian calzones and pizza accented with flavorful cheeses and Mediterranean vegetables.

Under the Huppah and Over the Stove

I had just met Daryl's cousin and her husband a couple of days before. And now, standing a few feet apart, they waited for us. Beyond them was a narrow lake shouldering the mountainside. The just-fallen sun still glowed behind the hill, and close family and friends gathered, holding candles to press back the fading light.

Nita's pale complexion shone against her sapphire blue jacket and skirt, and Joe's dark suit brought out the sparkle in his eyes. They both grasped brass poles that held up two of the four corners of a Jewish prayer shawl, the huppah under which I (having converted to Judaism about a year before) had just arrived with Daryl to be married. Nita stood just beyond my left shoulder, Joe beyond my right, looking on, waiting for us, and smiling.

A few months later, they waited for us again—this time at the front door of their Philadelphia home. Though Daryl had visited often over the years, this was my first time. And I had goals. First, I wanted to know them better because I could already tell from how they smiled under the huppah that they were warm and kind people. But also, I wanted to experience Jewishness in the context of the family just being together, the way it shows itself in life's smaller moments. I had been Jewish for a while, but I still sought my own special connection to the culture, something that went beyond the rituals. So there I stood. We plunged in—a sea of arms, laughs, dogs, luggage, and dueling video cameras trying to capture the commotion. And, wait a minute! Was that garlic and tomatoes? Finding out what these old Italian aromas were doing there became my third goal.

The family shepherded us to the spacious family room. I sank into a spot on the plush and plump blue sofa close to the fireplace, where a crackling wood fire chased the January day's chill from the room. While we were talking, Nita brought trays of snacks and Joe took drink orders. Daryl asked for a Yuengling because he thought that's what Joe always had in stock. Joe paused and smiled, then disappeared. Fifteen minutes later, he walked in through the front door with the beer he had just run out and bought at the store. And that was just the beginning of the hospitality in their household.

The conversation naturally turned to food. Even as she plied us with cheese and crackers, Nita warned against getting full—I'm making lasagna, she said. She knew Daryl adored her lasagna, and being the consummate Jewish mother, she made exactly what she knew her guest loved the most. Already impressed, my eyes grew wider when she continued. We're also having soup, salad, meatballs, and garlic toast—and you need to save room for dessert.

I followed Nita to the kitchen. I watched my Jewish cousin-in-law sprinkle Locatelli brand Pecorino Romano grated cheese over the layered pasta casserole, as a pot of tomato sauce simmered on the stove and a baking sheet of bread slices awaited butter and garlic on the counter. I asked about her recipes. Nita, already a great cook, discovered Italian food when she met Joe. When Nita and Joe married, Joe's mother, a Catholic immigrant from northern Italy, passed down recipes, lessons, and tips. Nita learned the family's tomato gravy (sauce) and other pasta and meat dishes, as well as soups, like the one for today—rolled pasta in clear chicken broth. The Italian recipes became her favorites, and, in turn, her family's favorites. Nita's Jewish father Rocky loved her lasagna so much that he stopped ordering it in restaurants. It would never be as good, he had declared.

Nita joked about how the Italian began to merge with the Jewish, albeit unintentionally. When she made Jewish noodle kugels, Joe and the kids often doused theirs with tomato gravy. Nita still loved the Jewish foods from her childhood, too, getting cravings for potato latkes or enjoying a batch of fried matzah. Her grandfather and much of the family had assimilated to American life very well, and her connection to her Jewish heritage maintained itself mostly through food and family. I understood. My Italian side also blended into American life so well that my connection to it was mostly through foods like what Nita was making right then.

We took seats at the large, oval wood dining room table, set as if for a holiday with a white tablecloth and fine dishes and glasses. Joe sat at the head of the table, delightedly directing the traffic of food-filled bowls and platters flowing in from the kitchen. Nita, personifying the Jewish mother/young Italian nonna, silently surveyed the table to see what anyone might need. Channeling age-old traditions of both Jewish and Italian hospitality, Joe and Nita made sure everyone had more than enough and exactly what they wanted.

After we cleared the dinner dishes, Nita disappeared to her pantry. She returned carrying a homemade cheesecake, another of her specialties. Desserts were her favorite part of dining, another thing we had in common. I watched her slice the sour cream-topped cake and knew even before my first bite that it was the perfect ending to the feast. By following her savory Italian dinner with a sweet dessert originating from New York Jewish delis, Nita made the whole event a warm and graceful embrace of the cultures of both her Jewish and Italian families.

As Daryl and I drove home, I started looking forward to creating my own Jewish-Italian kitchen. The next time I made lasagna, I imagined Nita right there over my shoulder, again waiting for me and smiling.

Dough

Extra-virgin olive oil

1 envelope active dry yeast (about 2¼ teaspoons)

1 cup very warm water (105 to 110 degrees)

2 tablespoons sugar

1½ teaspoons salt

4 eggs with one yolk reserved for the topping, room temperature (see note)

⅓ cup unsalted butter (or margarine or oil), softened (see note)

5 to 6 cups bread flour, plus additional for the work surface

Topping

Reserved egg yolk from dough recipe

Pinch of salt

1 teaspoon cold water

2½ to 3 teaspoons poppy or sesame seeds

Challah

Here's my mom's challah recipe that she received from a friend. It remains my favorite. The classic Jewish braided bread gains golden richness from eggs, and there's really nothing like it hot out of the oven. Butter gives this version exceptional flavor and texture, but if you need a more traditional nondairy challah, substitute margarine or oil for the butter. There are several ways you can braid your dough (see next page), but don't worry, even if you simply twist it in a knot, it will look fine and taste just as delicious.

Coat a large bowl with olive oil and set aside.

Dissolve the yeast and the warm water in a separate large bowl, about 5 minutes. Add the sugar, salt, 3 whole eggs and 1 egg white, and butter. Stir in 2½ cups of the flour to combine ingredients well. Add 2½ more cups of flour and mix well. Add additional flour as needed to form a cohesive dough.

Transfer to a floured surface. Knead for about 10 minutes, until the dough is smooth and elastic. Place the dough in the oiled bowl, remove it, turn it over, and place it (oiled side up) back in the bowl. Cover with plastic wrap and let rise until doubled, about 1½ to 2 hours.

Uncover the dough and press down on the middle to deflate it. Cover and let the dough rest for a few minutes.

Line a baking sheet with parchment paper.

Divide the dough in half. Return one half to the bowl and cover. Transfer the other half to a lightly floured surface and braid it (see options on next page). Transfer to the parchment-lined baking sheet. Repeat with remaining dough.

Lightly beat reserved egg yolk, a pinch of salt, and 1 teaspoon cold water to combine. Brush loaves with egg mixture and sprinkle liberally with poppy or sesame seeds. Gently cover the loaves with plastic wrap coated with oil or cooking spray. Let rise about 45 minutes, until loaves are puffy and nearly doubled.

Meanwhile, preheat the oven to 400 degrees.

Bake 14 to 20 minutes until loaves are well browned on top and bottom and sound hollow when tapped. Remove and transfer to a wire rack. Enjoy warm if possible.

Yield: Two large loaves (Dairy with butter; Pareve with margarine or oil)

Note: To bring cold eggs to room temperature, immerse them in a bowl of very warm tap water for about 2 minutes. To soften cold butter or margarine, cover loosely and place in microwave. Heat on very low power for 10 seconds at a time until just starting to soften—it should be between 65 and 67 degrees.

Braiding Options

THREE-STRAND BRAID

Divide the dough into 3 equal pieces. Roll each piece into a 12-inch rope. Align the ends, pinch them together, and braid the ropes (picking up the leftmost strand and crossing it over the middle strand, then the rightmost strand crossing over the middle, and so forth), pinching the ends to seal.

DOUBLE-LAYER THREE-STRAND BRAID

Layering two three-strand braids is an easy way to dress up the braid. Divide dough into 2 pieces, one piece about $2/3$ of the dough, the other piece $1/3$ of the dough. Divide the larger piece into 3 equal pieces. Roll each of those three into a 12-inch rope. Braid ropes together, pinch ends to seal. Divide small piece of dough into 3 pieces and roll each into a 10-inch rope. Braid and seal. Then place the smaller braid on top of the larger braid and press lightly. Gently seal together at ends.

SIX-STRAND BRAID

This makes a bakery-style intricate and elegant single-level braid. Don't worry about perfection; once the bread is baked, it will be difficult to detect a missing twist or two.

Divide the dough into 6 equal pieces and roll evenly into strands approximately 12 inches long. Arrange the strands side-by-side vertically. Squeeze top ends together firmly. Then:

1. Take leftmost strand and place it to the right over 2 strands and down the center.
2. Take the strand second from the right and place it over the top of all the other strands so that it is on the far left.
3. Take the rightmost strand and place it to the left over 2 strands and down the center.
4. Take the strand that is now second from the left and place it over the top of all the other strands so that it is on the far right.
5. Repeat the pattern.

You should always be working with the 4 outermost strands. When you have braided all the dough, pinch the ends together firmly.

Dough

Cooking spray or extra-virgin olive oil for coating the bowl and plastic wrap

$1/2$ cup rum

$1/2$ cup (generous) dark raisins

1 envelope active dry yeast (about $2^1/4$ teaspoons)

1 cup very warm water (105 to 110 degrees)

$1/2$ cup sugar

4 eggs (with one yolk reserved for topping), room temperature

$1/3$ cup unsalted butter (or margarine or oil), softened

1 teaspoon vanilla extract

$5^1/2$ to $6^1/2$ cups bread flour, plus additional for work surface

$1^1/2$ teaspoons salt

Filling

$1/2$ cup light brown sugar, packed

$1^1/4$ teaspoons ground cinnamon

2 tablespoons unsalted butter or margarine, melted

$1/4$ teaspoon vanilla extract

Egg Wash

Reserved egg yolk from dough recipe

Pinch of salt

1 teaspoon cold water

Rosh Hashanah Challah with Cinnamon and Raisins

Challah for the Jewish New Year is special—round to celebrate the circle of life and sweet (typically with raisins) in the hope of a sweet year. For the occasion, I make what I call my cinnamon roll challah, with rum-soaked raisins (an homage to Italian desserts featuring rum) and a pretty swirl of brown sugar and cinnamon inside. The loaves are large; you can freeze one to bake later if you like (see note).

Coat a large bowl with cooking spray or olive oil and set aside.

Heat rum in the microwave or on stovetop until hot. Pour over raisins to submerge them completely. Let stand about 10 minutes. Drain and discard the rum, and pat the raisins dry. Set aside.

Dissolve the yeast and the warm water in a large bowl, about 5 minutes. Mix in the sugar, 3 whole eggs and the egg white, butter, and vanilla. Stir in 2½ cups of the flour and the salt, and combine well. Then add 2½ more cups of flour and mix well. Add more flour as needed to form a cohesive dough.

Transfer the dough to a lightly floured surface, and knead for about 10 minutes until smooth and elastic. Press the dough into a large thick disk, and insert a handful of the raisins, spaced apart. Fold the dough over the raisins, and flatten again; continue inserting raisins this way until all are incorporated and well distributed.

Place the dough in the oiled bowl, then lift out, turn over, and place it (oiled side up) back in the bowl. Cover with plastic wrap and set in a warm place to rise until doubled, about 1½ to 2 hours.

Uncover the dough and press down on the middle to deflate. Cover and let rest for a few minutes.

Line a baking sheet with parchment paper and set aside. Prepare the filling by stirring together the brown sugar and cinnamon. In a separate bowl, combine the vanilla extract and the melted butter.

Divide the dough in half. Return one half to the bowl and cover. Place the other half on a lightly floured surface. Roll out to a large rectangle, about

20 inches long by 9 to 10 inches wide. Brush a thin layer of the butter over the dough. Then sprinkle with half the brown sugar mixture.

Starting at one long edge of the dough, roll it (jelly-roll style) gently but firmly to the other edge. Press the seam and ends to seal. Gently pull and roll this log until it is about 24 inches long, keeping the original thickness on one end and gradually narrowing the other end. Twine the narrow end around the larger end to make a large pinwheel. Press the loose end to seal. Gently press down on the top of the entire loaf to level it.

Transfer to prepared baking sheet. Repeat with remaining dough. Prepare the egg wash by lightly beating the reserved egg yolk, a pinch of salt, and 1 teaspoon cold water to combine. Brush on shaped loaves. Gently cover the loaves with oiled plastic wrap and let rise about 45 minutes, until nearly doubled.

Halfway through the rise, preheat the oven to 375 degrees.

Bake for 20 minutes, and then reduce heat to 350 degrees. Bake another 15 to 18 minutes, until loaf sounds hollow when tapped (the interior should be between 185 and 190 degrees). Some of the sugar mixture might seep out and create a sweet undercrust, which I consider ideal. Serve the same day or freeze.

Yield: Two large loaves (Dairy with butter; Pareve with margarine or oil)

Note: Both regular and sweet challah can be prepared up until right before the baking step and then frozen for up to four weeks. To bake, place unwrapped frozen loaf on a baking sheet lined with parchment paper. Cover with oiled plastic wrap to thaw (2 to 3 hours). Bake as directed.

Challah French Toast

1 large egg

2 tablespoons unsalted butter, melted

Extra unsalted butter for frying

³/₄ cup milk

2¹/₂ teaspoons vanilla extract

2 tablespoons sugar

¹/₃ cup all-purpose flour

¹/₄ teaspoon cinnamon

¹/₄ teaspoon salt

5 slices (³/₄-inches-thick) challah bread (preferably day-old)

8 ounces mascarpone cheese creamed with honey and ground cinnamon to taste

Leftover challah—homemade or store-bought—turns out tender, slightly sweet French toast. A topping of mascarpone cheese creamed with honey and cinnamon gives it an Italian touch. This recipe, adapted from Cook's Illustrated (May/June 1997), creates a nice coating that is not too eggy.

Preheat a large heavy skillet (cast-iron if possible) over medium heat until very hot. Meanwhile, beat egg lightly in a shallow dish. Whisk in melted butter to incorporate, followed by the milk and vanilla, and then the sugar, flour, cinnamon, and salt. Whisk until the batter is smooth.

Soak bread slices in the batter until just saturated, about 30 to 60 seconds per side, depending on the density of the bread. Avoid soaking to the point of the bread's tearing. Remove bread, allowing excess batter to drip back into the dish. Repeat with remaining slices.

Melt 1 tablespoon of butter in the hot skillet, swirling to coat. Cook battered bread slices (as many as will fit without crowding), turning until both sides are golden brown, 1 to 2 minutes on the first side and about 1 minute on the second side. Repeat with remaining slices, melting about 1 tablespoon of butter in the skillet before each new batch. Serve as soon as possible with mascarpone topping.

Yield: 5 slices (Dairy)

Note: If needed, keep slices warm by placing finished slices on a wire rack over a rimmed baking sheet in a preheated 250-degree oven.

The Jewish Girl's Garlic Toast

1 loaf Italian bread, day old

4 tablespoons (¹/₂ stick) salted butter, room temperature (soft enough to spread easily)

Garlic powder

Regular salt

Paprika

I thought I knew how to make garlic bread. Then I had my Jewish cousin-in-law Nita's version. It's buttery, well seasoned with salt and garlic, and crisp outside but almost pillowy inside. There's usually a (somewhat) friendly argument over who gets the last piece. Bread that has been stored in a sealed bag for at least one day makes the best toast. Use salted butter for this recipe.

Preheat the broiler. Adjust the oven rack to the middle position.

Slice the bread into ³/₄-inch-thick slices. Place cut-side down in a single layer directly on a baking sheet. Spread a generous layer of butter on top of each slice. Sprinkle generously with garlic powder and then a light layer of salt and paprika. Broil for 2 to 5 minutes, until lightly browned on top. Remove and serve immediately.

Yield: 8 to 14 slices (Dairy)

Parmesan Herb Bread

When I want to make bread for a special dinner, this is one of my favorites. For not much trouble at all, you get a beautiful loaf bursting with herb and cheese flavor. Adapted from a recipe in Cooking Light, *October 1998.*

Dough

1 envelope (about 2¼ teaspoons) active dry yeast

2 teaspoons sugar

1 cup very warm water (105 to 110 degrees)

2½ cups bread flour, plus more as needed for dough and work surface

1 teaspoon chopped fresh rosemary

1 teaspoon dried basil

½ teaspoon dried oregano

½ teaspoon dried thyme

1¼ teaspoons kosher salt

Extra-virgin olive oil

Topping

3½ tablespoons freshly grated Parmesan cheese

1 teaspoon chopped fresh rosemary

⅛ teaspoon garlic powder

Dissolve the yeast and sugar in the warm water in a large bowl, about 5 minutes. Stir in 1 cup of the flour and the herbs and salt until well incorporated. Then add the remaining 1½ cups of flour, adding more as needed to make a slightly sticky but workable dough.

Transfer the dough to a lightly floured surface and knead for 8 to 10 minutes, until smooth and elastic. Form into a large ball.

Coat a bowl with olive oil. Place the dough in the bowl, remove it, turn it over, and place it (oiled side up) back in the bowl. Cover and let rise for approximately 1½ hours, until doubled.

Uncover dough and deflate by pressing down on the middle. Let rest for 5 to 10 minutes. Meanwhile, preheat the oven to 350 degrees. Cover a baking sheet with parchment paper. Make the topping by combining the cheese, rosemary, and garlic powder.

Transfer dough to a lightly floured surface. Rub all over with olive oil to give it a thin coat, and shape into a loaf about 12 inches long. Place loaf on prepared baking sheet. Sprinkle the cheese mixture over the top and press some into the sides.

Bake for 30 to 40 minutes, until lightly browned and loaf sounds hollow when tapped. Transfer to a wire rack to cool.

Yield: 1 loaf (Dairy)

Calzones with Sun-Dried Tomatoes and Three Cheeses

Dough

1 envelope active dry yeast
(about 2¼ teaspoons)

1½ cups very warm water (105
to 110 degrees)

1½ teaspoons salt

2 tablespoons extra-virgin olive
oil, plus additional for coating the
bowl

4 cups bread flour, plus additional
as needed

Cooking spray

Filling and Calzones

2 cups shredded low-moisture
mozzarella cheese

1 cup shredded extra-sharp
provolone cheese

½ cup whole-milk ricotta cheese
(drained if runny)

1 cup drained and chopped sun-
dried tomatoes (packed in oil)

¾ cup loosely packed fresh basil
leaves, chopped

¼ teaspoon crushed red pepper
flakes

Freshly ground black pepper

Extra-virgin olive oil

Kosher salt

2 tablespoons freshly grated
Parmesan cheese for garnish
(optional)

1 cup marinara sauce for dipping
(optional; use jarred or see next
recipe)

The three cheeses in these calzones ("trouser legs") make them deliciously rich, and the sun-dried tomatoes offer a contrasting burst of flavor (and sub for the meat used in a traditional calzone and the anchovies used in a Jewish-Italian one). Although these folded-over pizzas are at their best hot out of the oven, they also work baked in advance, frozen, and reheated. For baking, use a light-colored baking sheet if possible (you can also use a pizza stone; see the note). If using a dark-colored baking sheet, bake the calzones at 475 degrees and watch bottoms carefully.

To make the dough, dissolve the yeast in the warm water in a large bowl, about 5 minutes. Stir in salt and olive oil, and then stir in all but half a cup of the flour. Gradually mix in additional flour as needed to form a workable dough. Transfer the mixture to a floured board, and knead for about 10 minutes until the dough is smooth and elastic. Form into a large ball.

Lightly coat a large bowl with olive oil. Place the dough in the bowl, then remove the ball, turn it over, and place it (oiled side up) back in the bowl. Cover the bowl and let rise until doubled, about 1½ hours.

Uncover dough and deflate by pressing in the middle with your fist. Using lightly floured hands, divide and roll the dough into six balls. Place the balls on a sheet of plastic wrap coated with cooking spray and cover loosely with another sheet of wrap coated with spray. Let stand 15 to 20 minutes. Uncover and press each ball into a thick disk and let stand 5 more minutes. (These steps will make the dough easier to roll.)

Meanwhile, preheat the oven to 500 degrees. Line a large baking sheet with parchment paper and set aside.

Make the filling by combining the mozzarella, provolone, ricotta, sun-dried tomatoes, basil, red pepper flakes, and black pepper in a medium bowl.

Place 1 dough ball on a floured surface, and gently roll or press to form an 8-inch-wide circle. Spread about 2/3 cup of filling on the bottom half of the circle, leaving a 1-inch border.

Carefully fold the top down, leaving about 1/2 inch of the bottom layer uncovered. Fold that bottom lip up around the edge, crimping firmly to seal. With a sharp knife, slash the top in several places to allow steam to escape. Brush top with olive oil and sprinkle lightly with kosher salt. Transfer to prepared baking sheet.

Repeat with remaining dough. Bake until golden brown, 8 to 12 minutes (if browning too quickly on the bottom, reduce heat to 475 degrees). Transfer to a wire rack.

Serve warm or at room temperature. If desired, pass grated Parmesan cheese and marinara sauce at the table.

Refrigerate or freeze leftovers. Reheat (thaw first if frozen) in a 375-degree oven until warmed through, 6 to 12 minutes.

Yield: 6 large calzones (Dairy)

Note: If using a pizza stone, insert it when you preheat the oven. Place prepped calzones on parchment paper trimmed to fit the stone and transfer both parchment and calzones to stone for baking (you will probably need to bake in two or more batches).

Quick Marinara for Calzones

When I need a quick, good, all-purpose tomato sauce, this is what I make. It works as a dipping sauce for calzones or for topping pasta or pizza.

Heat a thin layer of olive oil in a medium saucepan over medium heat. Add the garlic and red pepper flakes, and sauté 1 minute, until garlic is fragrant. Stir in oregano and tomatoes. Simmer 15 to 20 minutes. Stir in basil if using and remove sauce from heat.

Yield: 3 cups sauce (Pareve)

Extra-virgin olive oil

2 garlic cloves, pressed through a garlic press or minced

1/8 teaspoon crushed red pepper flakes

1/8 teaspoon dried oregano

1 can (28 ounces) crushed tomatoes

2 tablespoons chopped fresh basil (optional)

Dough

Extra-virgin olive oil

2 envelopes (¼ ounce each)
active dry yeast

1¼ cups very warm water
(105 to 110 degrees)

1 tablespoon honey

4 cups all-purpose or bread flour
plus additional as needed (see
note)

2 teaspoons kosher salt

Topping

2 large heads of garlic

Kosher salt

Extra-virgin olive oil

3 cans (14 ounces each)
artichoke hearts packed in water,
drained and quartered

¼ cup chopped oil-packed sun-
dried tomatoes, drained of excess
oil

3 cups (about ¾ to 1 pound)
shredded smoked Gouda cheese

¾ cup finely grated Parmesan
cheese

Pizza with Roasted Artichokes, Garlic, and Smoked Gouda

Topped with roasted artichokes, a favored vegetable in the cuisine of Italy's Jews, and sweet roasted garlic along with sun-dried tomatoes and smoky Gouda cheese, this pizza has deep flavor and pleasant chewy textures. I use parchment paper for baking, either on a pizza stone or a baking sheet. This recipe creates three 10-inch pizzas.

Coat a large bowl with olive oil and set aside.

Dissolve the yeast in the warm water in a separate large bowl, about 5 minutes. Stir in 3 tablespoons of olive oil and the honey. Add 2 cups of the flour and stir to combine. Sprinkle an additional cup of flour over the batter, and then sprinkle on the kosher salt. Mix well. Add flour until a cohesive dough forms.

Transfer dough to a lightly floured surface, and knead for 11 to 12 minutes, adding flour as needed to keep the dough workable, until dough is smooth and elastic. Form into a ball.

Place the dough in the oiled bowl. Remove it, turn it over, and place it (oiled side up) back in the bowl. Cover with plastic wrap or a kitchen towel, and set aside to rise until doubled, about 1 hour.

Meanwhile, prepare the garlic and artichokes. Preheat the oven to 375 degrees. Remove as much of the outer papery skin from the garlic heads as possible without breaking the heads apart. Place the garlic in a small baking dish, add 4 tablespoons of water and a sprinkling of salt, then drizzle with about 1 tablespoon of olive oil (there should be enough liquid to form a thin layer on the bottom of the dish). Cover tightly.

In a roasting or jelly-roll pan, toss the artichoke hearts with olive oil to coat and arrange in a single layer (use 2 pans if necessary). Bake the garlic and artichokes for approximately 45 minutes, stirring the artichokes a few times and basting the garlic with the oil-and-water mixture at the halfway point. When done, the garlic will be soft throughout and the artichoke hearts will be lightly browned. Remove and set aside to cool.

Turn the oven to 500 degrees, and preheat a pizza stone if using.

Deflate the dough by pressing down on the middle, then cover and let it rest for a few minutes. Coat a large piece of plastic wrap with olive oil or cooking spray. With lightly floured hands, divide the dough into 3 similar-sized pieces and roll into balls. Place the balls on the oiled wrap and cover with a kitchen towel or plastic wrap coated with oil or cooking spray. Let rest for 10 minutes.

Tear off three large pieces of parchment paper. With lightly floured hands, remove one dough ball. Flatten and then gently stretch the dough into a disk. If the dough is difficult to work with, let it rest a moment. Stretch to a 6- or 7-inch circle with a lip around the edges. Place on a sheet of the parchment paper and press to an approximate 10-inch circle.

Brush with olive oil and sprinkle lightly with kosher salt. On the crust, arrange 1/3 of the artichokes, 1/3 of the garlic cloves (squeezed from the papery lining), 1/3 of the tomatoes, and then 1/3 of each of the cheeses. Trim the parchment so that about 2 inches extend past the edge of the pizza. Repeat with the remaining dough.

Transfer the pizza to the hot stone in the oven or to a baking sheet. If you want to use two baking sheets, you can bake 2 pizzas at once while you finish the 3rd.

Bake for 7 to 12 minutes, until the crust and bottom are golden brown and the cheese is melted. Remove and let pizzas rest about 3 minutes before slicing and serving.

Yield: Three 10-inch pizzas (Dairy)

Note: Bread flour makes the crust a bit chewier, all-purpose flour makes it a bit crispier. Both are equally good.

Extra-virgin olive oil

2 envelopes (¼ ounce each) active dry yeast

2 cups very warm water (105 to 110 degrees)

1 teaspoon sugar

6 to 7 cups bread flour, plus extra for the work surface

1½ tablespoons kosher salt, plus additional for onion topping and sprinkling

3 tablespoons dried minced onion

1 egg yolk mixed with 1 tablespoon cold water

1 tablespoon poppy seeds (optional)

Bialys

Bialys originated in Bialystok, Poland; they were brought to the United States by Jewish immigrants in the early 1900s. Cousin to the bagel, bialys are fun, small round breads with an indent rather than a hole— all the better for cradling the traditional seasonings like onion, salt, and poppy seeds. They freeze well and provide a great base for mini pizzas (see next recipe).

Coat a large bowl with olive oil and set aside.

Dissolve the yeast in the warm water in a separate bowl, about 5 minutes. Add the sugar. Stir in about 5½ cups of the flour and 1½ tablespoons kosher salt. Continue adding flour until the dough holds together. Transfer to a floured board, and knead for about 10 minutes, until smooth (the dough will be very dense). Form into a ball.

Place the dough in the oiled bowl, then remove it, turn it over, and place it (oiled side up) back in the bowl. Cover with plastic wrap and let rise until doubled, about 2 hours.

Uncover dough and press down the middle to deflate. Divide the dough into 16 equal pieces and roll into balls. Place on a lightly floured or parchment-lined surface, cover with oiled plastic wrap, and let rise until nearly doubled (about 1½ to 2 hours).

Prepare the onion topping by placing the dried onion in a small dish and covering with 1/2 cup very warm water. Let stand for at least 15 minutes. Drain any excess water, and toss with 1/2 tablespoon olive oil and 1/2 teaspoon kosher salt.

Adjust the oven rack to the second-to-top position, and place a baking stone or a cookie sheet on the rack. Preheat the oven to 475 degrees. Cut a piece of parchment paper roughly the size of the stone or pan and set aside on the counter.

Take one ball of dough (keeping the rest covered), and flatten on a lightly floured surface. Stretch with fingers to 4 to 5 inches in diameter. Gently pull the center and then press very firmly with thumbs until the dough holds a thin, 2-inch-wide indent (the thinner the indent, the more likely it will keep its shape during baking). The bialy will look somewhat flat, but the edges will puff up during baking.

Place on the parchment, and brush with egg yolk mixture, sprinkle lightly with kosher salt, fill indent with about 1/2 to 1 teaspoon of the onion mixture, and sprinkle all over with poppy seeds if using. Repeat with remaining balls.

When the parchment is full, slide it with the bialys onto the hot stone or baking sheet, and bake until bialys are lightly browned, 9 to 12 minutes. Remove to a wire rack. Repeat with remaining batches.

Serve warm or at room temperature with butter, cream cheese, or any bread spread.

Yield: 16 bialys (Pareve)

Bialy Pizzas

If I didn't know better, I'd insist bialys were made for becoming pizza. The flattened center nicely contains a spoonful of tomato sauce and a slice of fresh mozzarella cheese (or any other topping) on a base of yeasty dough. Cut in quarters, bialy pizzas make a quick, festive party appetizer melding popular Jewish and Italian foods.

Preheat the oven to 375 degrees. Line a baking sheet with parchment paper. Place the bialys on the sheet. Drop approximately 1 tablespoon of sauce into the center and top with a slice of fresh mozzarella.

Bake until the cheese is melted, about 15 minutes.

Yield: 6 bialy pizzas (Dairy)

6 bialys

1 cup Quick Marinara Sauce (see recipe on p. 73) or any jarred pizza sauce

6 small slices fresh mozzarella cheese, patted dry

2 medium baking potatoes, peeled and quartered

1 envelope (about 2¼ teaspoons) active dry yeast

1½ cups very warm water (105 to 110 degrees)

Extra-virgin olive oil

2 teaspoons kosher salt, plus additional for cooking potatoes and topping the bread

4 to 5 cups bread flour, plus additional for the work surface

2 fingerling or other small potatoes, peeled and sliced paper thin with a vegetable peeler

Freshly ground black pepper

2½ tablespoons fresh rosemary leaves

Focaccia with Potato and Rosemary

Potato, a vegetable popular in Jewish knishes, offers an interesting dimension to the Italian dimpled flatbread focaccia. In my version, cooked potato boosts taste and moisture in the bread and sliced potato on top gives crispness and still more potato flavor—all complemented by fresh rosemary.

Cook the 2 baking potatoes in salted, boiling water until tender, 20 to 25 minutes. Drain, cool slightly, and press through a potato ricer or finely grate. Measure approximately 1⅓ cups; set aside any remainder for another use.

Dissolve the yeast in the warm water in a large bowl, about 5 minutes. Stir in riced or grated potato, 2 tablespoons of olive oil, and the 2 teaspoons of kosher salt, and stir to combine. Add 2 cups of flour and stir to make a loose batter. Stir in 2 more cups of flour—and more if needed—to make a thick dough.

Transfer dough to a floured surface, and knead for 7 to 9 minutes until dough is smooth and elastic, adding flour as needed to keep the dough workable but still quite moist and sticky.

Coat a large bowl with olive oil. Shape the dough into a ball and place the ball in the bowl, remove it, turn it over, and place it (oiled side up) back in the bowl. Cover with plastic wrap and let rise until doubled, about 1 hour.

Deflate the dough by pressing down on the middle. Let rest, loosely covered, for 5 minutes. Line a 17-by-12-inch jelly-roll pan with parchment paper. Transfer the dough to the pan, and using fingers moistened with water, gently spread the dough to fill the pan. If the dough resists, let it rest a few minutes and try again.

Cover dough with oiled plastic wrap, and let rise until dough is puffy and approximately doubled in volume, about 1 hour. About halfway through, preheat the oven to 425 degrees.

Uncover the dough. Wet fingers with water and press them into the dough at 1- to 2-inch intervals to create dimples. Brush on about 2 tablespoons of olive oil, allowing some oil to pool in the dimples. In a

separate bowl, toss the potato slices with olive oil and freshly ground black pepper to taste. Place potato slices on top of dough in a single layer. Sprinkle with rosemary and kosher salt to taste.

Bake until top and bottom are golden brown and slightly crisp, 25 to 30 minutes. Remove from oven and transfer to a wire rack to cool. Slice into squares and serve warm or at room temperature the same day. Or cool completely, wrap well, and freeze.

Yield: One 17-by-12-inch loaf of focaccia (about 15 large pieces) (Pareve)

Pita Bread

1½ teaspoons active dry yeast

1 cup very warm water (105 to 110 degrees)

1 tablespoon extra-virgin olive oil, plus additional for oiling the bowl

2½ teaspoons kosher salt

2 cups bread flour

1 cup white whole wheat flour (see note)

Pita can be found all over Israel and the Middle Eastern region, where it originated. Like so many other baked goods, homemade pita far surpasses anything you might buy at the grocery store. Here's the best part—making bread with a pocket might sound complicated, but it's surprisingly easy.

Dissolve the yeast in the warm water in a large bowl, about 5 minutes. Lightly coat a separate large bowl with olive oil.

Stir in the salt and 1 tablespoon of olive oil to the yeast mixture, then stir in the flour to make a barely sticky dough. If the dough is too wet, add more flour. If too dry, add more water.

Transfer to a lightly floured surface and knead for 5 to 7 minutes, until smooth and elastic. Form a ball. Place the dough in the oiled bowl, remove the dough, turn it over, and place it (oiled side up) back in the bowl. Cover with plastic wrap and let rise until doubled, 1½ to 2 hours.

Place a baking stone or baking sheet in the oven. Preheat to 500 degrees.

Uncover the dough and deflate it. Let it rest for 5 minutes, then divide it into 6 to 12 pieces (depending on the size pita desired).

On a lightly floured surface, press each dough ball into a disk. With a rolling pin, roll into a smooth 4- to 5-inch circle (if 12 pieces) or 6- to 7-inch circle (if 6 pieces). Avoid having creases or seams, which will inhibit the pocket from forming during baking. Set aside finished disks, covered, in a single layer.

Place as many pita as will fit on the hot baking stone or sheet in the oven. Bake until the pita puff up and bottoms just start to brown, 2 to 4 minutes. Remove the pita to a wire rack. Repeat with remaining dough.

If freezing, wrap individually in wax paper and place in freezer-proof bags immediately upon cooling.

Yield: 12 small or 6 large pitas (Pareve)

Note: White whole wheat flour adds a mild nutty flavor. You can use all white bread flour if you prefer. Note that different flours absorb water differently, so changing the flour type or proportion might affect the amount of water needed.

Pita Crisps

Pita (fresh or slightly stale) can make a quick and easy transformation to a lightly spiced crisp—great for snacking, dipping, or serving alongside salads.

Preheat the oven to 350 degrees.

Cut pita into wedges. Spread in a single layer on a baking sheet. Brush lightly with olive oil. Sprinkle with garlic powder, paprika, and kosher salt.

Bake until lightly browned, 15 to 20 minutes, and then turn pieces to brown the other side for a few more minutes. Remove.

Serve warm or at room temperature. Store in a closed container or a zip-top plastic bag.

Yield: 24 to 36 pita crisps (Pareve)

4 small- or medium-sized pita breads

Extra-virgin olive oil

Garlic powder

Paprika

Kosher salt

Chapter 5

Appetizers and Starters

Appetizers are the fun foods (or a fun drink)—fun to make, fun to serve, and fun to eat. I also treasure them for their versatility. Appetizers fulfill all sorts of duties—side dishes, desserts, snacks, and even dinner. We've been known to make meals of latkes, artichoke dip, or hummus. These selected recipes range from easy (sun-dried tomato spread or stuffed strawberries) to a little more involved (latkes), and from traditional (Italian eggplant caponata) to revisionist (a vegetarian version of Jewish chopped liver) to outside the box (white peach sangria, an oft-requested original recipe).

Reflections
SO NAMED

Recipes
JACOB FRIEDMAN'S POTATO LATKES

BAKED ARTICHOKE AND
PARMESAN DIP

ITALIAN SUN-DRIED TOMATO
AND OLIVE SPREAD

GRILLED CAPRESE SALAD SKEWERS

HUMMUS WITH TOASTED GARLIC

STUFFED CELERY

MY WHITE PEACH SANGRIA

EGGPLANT CAPONATA

VEGETARIAN PÂTÉ CROSTINI

STUFFED STRAWBERRIES
WITH CASHEWS

WALNUT CHICKEN PIROSHKIS

BERNEY THOMPSON

JACOB FRIEDMAN

So Named

Sometimes recipes are attached to a name. They become treasured not only for what they create but also for who created them. The recipe and the person become inseparable.

Two recipes are named in this collection.

One is for my dad, Berney. He loved food, especially sauce and pasta and sweets—my favorites, too. The food I most associate with him is his special tomato sauce along with meatballs. When he cooked the sauce and meatballs, the aroma worked its way into every nook and cranny in the house.

The other named recipe is for my grandfather-in-law, Jacob. Daryl associates the scent of chicken soup with going to his Grandpa Jacob's small house in Los Angeles. But I never met Jacob—the food I connect with him is latkes. Like Dad's sauce, the aroma of

Jacob's latkes permeates the house and lingers, a reminder of not just food, but of people and stories.

Jacob learned his latke recipe from his father in Poland. He'd make these potato pancakes for his wife, Dora, and young boys, Henry and David, using potatoes, onions, and eggs from their farm. Like other Jewish families, they especially enjoyed latkes at Hanukkah, the Jewish festival often celebrated with foods fried in oil.

In 1941, Jacob stopped making latkes because family life as he knew it ceased to exist. Their town of Brody, Poland, came under Nazi control. The Germans ordered Jews to report to stations for transport to camps; those who didn't comply were to be killed. Jacob knew well the rumors of what happened to Jews in ghettos and the nearby camps—Majdanek, Auschwitz-Birkenau, and Treblinka. With his sons' teacher Clara, he hatched a plan that he hoped would save them. They enlisted the help of a sympathetic Christian family, who hid Dora, the boys, and Clara in the attic of their barn. Jacob took cover a mile away in a hayloft. Hours of hiding in fear with little food, water, or daylight turned into days. And then weeks. And then months. And then a year and a half. But their strategy and perseverance saved their lives. When the Germans retreated, the Friedman family and Clara emerged to count themselves among just 100 surviving Jews in a town once the home of 15,000.

Although they faced many more hardships, they eventually followed paths to better lives. Jacob and Dora had another son, Allan, and the family immigrated to the United States. Jacob became a grandfather to Henry's three children and David's sons, Andrew and Daryl, and he made lots more latkes. Clara found her way to Israel and reunited with members of her own family. But the bonds formed during hiding remained, and decades later, Daryl's father, David, journeyed to Israel to find Clara again. One of his favorite recollections of that trip involves food. After twenty-six years, Clara remembered young David's favorite food from Poland, a calves' foot jelly called petcha. She made the dish and presented it when he walked through the door. Astonished and moved, he could hardly speak.

The recipe the Friedman family holds onto, though, is Jacob's latkes. David learned the recipe from Jacob and taught it to his son Daryl—who now retraces Jacob's footsteps in the kitchen every Hanukkah, starting with grating the potatoes by hand.

***

I retrace footsteps myself when I make my Dad's spicy tomato sauce. When the tomato mixture starts to bubble and I stir in the dried oregano and basil, I remember how Dad always seemed especially satisfied standing beside the stove and stirring spices into the oblong silver pot. However, like Jacob stopped making latkes for a time, my dad reached a point at which he stopped making his sauce.

My dad's life slowly became robbed of spice by an internal enemy—multiple sclerosis (MS). The autoimmune disease maliciously sets the body's own defenses against it—tricking the immune system into attacking the nerve endings along the spinal cord. The repeated assaults slowly strip the body of functions so easily taken for granted—eyesight, feeling in fingers and toes, and the ability to keep the body balanced enough to stand and walk without falling. The disease varies dramatically from person to person and even from month to month.

By the time my dad turned 40, it was clear that his disease was taking an aggressive track. In return, he applied his penchant for experimenting and problem solving to working around his growing limitations as best he could. He learned to use a walker and eventually a motorized wheelchair. He joined an experimental drug trial at the National Institutes of Health in the hope that a promising new treatment might be effective. But after a few months, before the doctors even told him, he knew—he was in the control group, getting nothing more than a placebo even as he forewent other drugs that had been helping him before the trial. His sacrifice, we could only hope, helped advance the painfully slow progress of finding an effective treatment for MS.

Complications from the disease finally claimed his life when he was only 50. He hadn't had nearly enough good days to enjoy his life with his wife, Sandra, or enjoy what he loved, such as fishing on the Juniata River, lounging in the sun, or making his sauce. And we hadn't had enough time to enjoy him and truly get to know the man with dark curly hair, the big grin, and the occasional sense of mischief. But he did leave behind examples of courage, perseverance, humor, and dedication to family. And also memories, like a great sauce recipe that I love to make and remember him by. Me, the tomatoes, the oregano and basil, and a houseful of Italian aromas, lingering awhile to keep me company.

5 medium russet or baking potatoes, peeled

1½ large onions, peeled

2 large eggs, lightly beaten

½ cup all-purpose flour

2 teaspoons salt, plus additional to taste

1 teaspoon ground black pepper, plus additional to taste

Canola or vegetable oil for frying

Jacob Friedman's Potato Latkes

This recipe from Daryl's grandfather Jacob offers a classically delicious take on the Jewish potato pancakes. We like the latkes small and crispy. Although it wouldn't be allowed according to Friedman tradition, you can use a food processor to grate the potatoes if you prefer. Traditionally they are served with sour cream or applesauce (we also enjoy them with vegetable dip). They can be made ahead (see note).

Using a handheld grater, finely grate the potatoes and onions, and mix well in a large bowl. Stir in the eggs and transfer the mixture to a fine-mesh strainer. Press to drain as much liquid as possible. Discard the liquid and return the potato mixture to the bowl. Stir in the flour, salt, and pepper.

Meanwhile, warm a large skillet (preferably cast-iron) over medium-high heat, and add about 1/4 inch of oil. When the oil is hot and begins to bubble (350 to 375 degrees), drop about one tablespoon of batter into the pan, and gently flatten to about 1/4-inch thick. Repeat with additional batter until the pan is full but the individual latkes don't touch one another. Nudge the pancakes with a spatula to ensure they don't stick to the bottom of the pan. When brown on the bottom, turn and brown the other side. Remove and drain between paper towels. Taste the cooked latkes, and add onion or salt and pepper to the remaining batter if needed.

Continue making batches with remaining batter. The latkes should be crispy and deep golden brown.

Serve immediately. Or to keep cooked latkes warm while you finish the rest, place them on a wire rack positioned over a cookie sheet in a 275-degree oven.

Yield: 24 to 32 potato pancakes (Pareve)

Note: You can make latkes in advance and freeze them. To serve, preheat oven to 350 degrees. Place frozen latkes on a wire rack placed over a baking sheet. Bake until crispy, about 20 minutes.

Baked Artichoke and Parmesan Dip

No wonder artichoke dip has been a party must for years—it's warm, creamy, substantial, subtly tangy, and really easy to make. Though not distinctly Jewish or Italian, the ingredients hit key highlights—artichokes (a popular ingredient in both cuisines), cheese, and garlic. I've had many versions, and this one given to me by my mom is the one I keep returning to.

Preheat the oven to 350 degrees.

Chop the artichokes into quarters or smaller. In a 2-quart baking dish, mix all the ingredients except the paprika until well combined. Level the top, and wipe any excess off the sides of the dish. Sprinkle liberally with paprika.

Bake for 30 minutes, until hot and bubbly. Serve hot right from the baking dish with crackers, Belgian endive pieces, or small bread slices for dipping.

The dip can be assembled in advance and refrigerated until ready to bake (allow for an extra 5 to 10 minutes' baking time).

Yield: About 4 cups (Dairy)

2 cans (14 ounces each) artichoke hearts packed in water, drained

1 cup mayonnaise

1 cup sour cream

1 cup grated Parmesan cheese

2 cloves garlic, pressed through a garlic press or minced

Dash of Worcestershire sauce

Paprika

1 cup pitted Kalamata olives

1 cup sun-dried tomatoes packed in oil, drained

Extra-virgin olive oil

Italian Sun-Dried Tomato and Olive Spread

The ease of this Italian specialty belies how dramatic it tastes. Serve it simply with bread, crackers, and even matzah, or try it as a relish with chicken or salmon.

Mince the olives and tomatoes by hand or in a small food processor. Then, by hand, gradually add olive oil as needed to make a spreadable mixture.

Refrigerate until ready to use. Serve cold or room temperature.

Yield: About 2 cups (Pareve)

Grilled Caprese Salad Skewers

10 wooden cocktail skewers (preferably 8 inches long), soaked in water for about 30 minutes

1 pint grape tomatoes or 2 pints cherry tomatoes

20 small balls of fresh mozzarella cheese packed in water, drained (or large pieces of mozzarella, cut into walnut-sized pieces)

20 fresh basil leaves

Extra-virgin olive oil

Kosher salt and freshly ground black pepper

Although I found recipes for grilled tomato salad in Jewish cookbooks, I skewered and grilled my favorite Italian tomato-basil-mozzarella salad mostly to have a festive but easy party appetizer. Quick grilling boosts the flavor and softens the cheese (a little runny is okay—good, actually); just be sure to remove the skewers from the heat before the mozzarella falls off.

Preheat a grill to medium.

Remove skewers from water and pat dry. For each skewer, thread tomato, mozzarella, and basil leaf, and end with a tomato (so typically 3 tomatoes, 2 mozzarella balls, and 2 leaves for each skewer). Brush with olive oil and sprinkle with salt and pepper. Transfer to grill (shaking off any excess oil before placing on the grate), and cook for 1 to 2 minutes, turning once with tongs, until cheese just starts to soften.

Yield: 10 skewers (Dairy)

2 tablespoons pine nuts

6 to 7 garlic cloves, separated but not peeled

1 can (16 ounces) chickpeas, drained with liquid reserved

1/3 cup tahini (sesame seed paste)

2 1/2 tablespoons fresh lemon juice

1/2 teaspoon kosher salt, plus more to taste

1/8 teaspoon of freshly ground black pepper or to taste

1/8 teaspoon (scant) ground red (cayenne) pepper

1/4 teaspoon (generous) cumin

Paprika

Extra-virgin olive oil

Hummus with Toasted Garlic

Although hummus is an Israeli/Middle Eastern specialty, the chickpeas (which appear in many Italian dishes) and the pine nuts (Italian pignoli) also make the dish naturally pan-Mediterranean. I prefer sweeter toasted garlic to complement the earthy bean and sesame flavors. Enjoy this the classic way—with fresh pita bread—but also as a vegetable or chip dip or as a sandwich spread.

Toast the pine nuts in small skillet over medium heat, stirring frequently, until lightly browned, 5 to 7 minutes. Remove to a small plate to cool. Add the garlic cloves to the skillet, and toast for about 10 minutes, turning often, until browned on at least one side and softened. Cool slightly and remove the paper skins.

Add the chickpeas to a blender and puree with the tahini, lemon juice, garlic, salt, black pepper, red pepper, and cumin, along with about 1/3 cup of the reserved chickpea liquid. Continue adding liquid and processing until smooth and creamy. Taste and add additional salt if needed. Refrigerate until ready to serve.

To serve, place in a wide, shallow bowl or plate and make a slight well. Sprinkle with the paprika, drizzle the center with olive oil, and top with the toasted pine nuts.

Hummus can be stored refrigerated for up to 4 days and also freezes well.

Yield: About 2 cups (Pareve)

Stuffed Celery

My dad's Italian family passed down this simple but beloved recipe, and my mom has been required to make it at family get-togethers ever since. In some Italian cookbooks, I've seen celery cooked and stuffed with ground meat, but we prefer the contrast of the crisp, fresh celery with the spiced extra-sharp Cheddar cheese.

1 pound celery hearts (one double package), ribs separated and washed

2 cups shredded extra-sharp Cheddar cheese

1 teaspoon spicy prepared mustard

1/4 cup light mayonnaise (preferably Miracle Whip dressing) (see note)

1/2 cup finely chopped walnuts

Trim and discard any leaves and the bottoms of the celery stalks. Cut stalks into approximately 3-inch pieces. Save pieces with very narrow or very flat cavities for another use. For crisper celery, soak the pieces in ice water for 10 to 20 minutes, then drain and dry.

In a small bowl, toss the mustard with the cheese. Add 1 tablespoon of the mayonnaise to the cheese mixture, blending gently with a fork. Add additional dressing, 1 tablespoon at a time, until the cheese mixture holds together in loose ball. Stir in the walnuts, and add more dressing if necessary.

Press the filling into the cavities of the celery pieces. Arrange stuffed celery on a plate, cover, and refrigerate until ready to serve.

Yield: 20 to 30 pieces (Dairy)

Note: We always used Miracle Whip, which offers a nice tanginess to the cheese filling. If using mayonnaise, season it lightly with a little paprika.

My White Peach Sangria

I would be in trouble if I didn't serve this drink at our summer parties. My chilled peachy sangria, reminiscent of the Italian Bellini, combines citrus and ripe peach flavors with white wine. Very ripe peaches are key.

3 ripe white peaches, peeled, pitted, and sliced (see note)

1 large juice orange, such as Valencia, washed

1 large lemon, washed

1/4 cup sugar

1/4 cup Triple Sec

1/4 cup peach liqueur

1 750 milliliter bottle of inexpensive Pinot Grigio or Sauvignon Blanc (or other light-bodied white wine)

Smash (or purée) the peaches, leaving some small chunks. Juice half the orange, and slice the other orange half and the lemon, removing seeds. Place the orange and lemon slices in the pitcher. Add sugar. Mash gently with a wooden spoon just enough to release juices and dissolve the sugar. Add the peach purée, orange juice, Triple Sec, liqueur, and wine. Stir well, and refrigerate at least 4 and up to 8 hours before serving.

Yield: About 6 servings (Pareve)

Note: Very ripe white peaches often peel very easily, but if they prove difficult, dunk them for 40 to 60 seconds in gently boiling water. Remove, let cool slightly, and peel.

Eggplant Caponata

2 medium eggplants (approximately 2 pounds), cut into 1/2-inch cubes (leave the skin on)

Kosher salt

Extra-virgin olive oil

1 large onion, chopped

2 bell peppers (preferably 1 red and 1 yellow), seeded and chopped

1/2 cup finely chopped celery

Freshly ground black pepper

3 garlic cloves, crushed or minced

1 can (14 1/2 ounces) diced tomatoes and juice

1 tablespoon capers, drained (optional)

1 tablespoon sugar

1 tablespoon red wine vinegar

1/4 cup shredded fresh basil

Roasting the eggplant gives a deeper flavor to this Sicilian eggplant dish—which might have Jewish travelers to thank for its origins. According to Jewish food historian Joan Nathan, in Italy eggplant has often been called a Jewish fruit, perhaps because Jewish merchants brought it to the region. A cross between a dip and a sauce, caponata goes equally well atop bread or crackers or over couscous or pasta.

Place eggplant cubes in a colander and toss well with 1/2 tablespoon kosher salt. Allow to drain for 45 to 60 minutes (or up to 3 hours). Rinse well, then press out liquid and pat dry with paper towels.

Preheat the oven to 475 degrees. Line a rimmed baking sheet with foil. Add the eggplant and toss with enough olive oil to lightly coat. Spread eggplant in a single layer and sprinkle with a generous teaspoon of kosher salt. Roast, stirring approximately every 10 minutes, until browned and tender, 20 to 30 minutes. (If the eggplant appears to be browning too quickly, reduce heat slightly and add a little more oil if needed.) Remove and set aside.

Heat a thin layer of olive oil in a large nonstick pan (preferably a Dutch oven) over medium-high heat. Add the onion, peppers, and celery, and season lightly with salt and pepper. Sauté until the vegetables begin to soften, 8 to 12 minutes (adding more oil if mixture dries out). Stir in the garlic and cook for about 30 seconds. Stir in the tomatoes, reserved eggplant, capers, sugar, black pepper (1/2 teaspoon or to taste), and vinegar. Simmer over low heat 5 to 10 minutes until the vegetables are cooked but not mushy. Stir in the basil during the last minute or so. The mixture will be thick. Taste and add salt if needed.

Best served at room temperature. Store in refrigerator.

Yield: About 4 1/2 cups (Pareve)

Extra-virgin olive oil

2 large sweet onions, sliced

Kosher salt and freshly ground black pepper

6 hardboiled eggs, peeled, with 3 yolks reserved for another use

2 cups walnut halves, lightly toasted in a skillet

2 cups green peas (frozen or fresh), cooked

¼ cup chopped Italian (flat leaf) parsley

20 to 24 very thin slices of narrow Italian bread or French baguette

¼ cup finely grated Parmesan cheese for garnish (optional)

Vegetarian Pâté Crostini

Jewish cuisine has its chopped liver and so does Italian (crostini, or little toasts, were traditionally served with chopped chicken livers). But vegetarian alternatives abound, and here's one based on my mother-in-law Gloria's recipe, featuring caramelized onions, toasted walnuts, and peas for meaty flavor without meat. You can serve this at Passover with matzah crackers. Omit the cheese topping if serving with meat dishes.

Heat a thin layer of olive oil in a large nonstick skillet over medium heat. Add the onions and season lightly with kosher salt and pepper. Cook slowly, turning often, until softened and lightly browned, 45 to 55 minutes.

Place the onions, eggs, walnuts, peas, parsley, and salt and pepper to taste in a food processor or blender (see note), and process until just a few small chunks remain. Refrigerate until ready to use.

When ready to assemble, toast the bread slices under the broiler until crisp.

Remove and brush the toasts with olive oil, and then spread on a spoonful of the pâté. Sprinkle with cheese and broil until cheese melts. Serve warm or at room temperature.

Yield: 3½ cups of vegetable spread; 20 to 24 crostini with plenty of extra spread leftover for crackers (Pareve without the cheese; Dairy with cheese)

Note: *Puréeing this thick mixture is a tough task for most blenders. If using a blender rather than a food processor, process half the mixture at a time, stopping and scraping the jar often to distribute the ingredients.*

Stuffed Strawberries with Cashews

8 ounces mascarpone cheese (see note)

1½ teaspoons honey or to taste

⅛ teaspoon (scant) nutmeg

1 pound strawberries, preferably medium to large

½ cup salted cashews, finely chopped

In search of a pretty and refreshing appetizer, I stuffed sweetened mascarpone cheese into strawberries and topped them with chopped cashews. Together these ingredients seem to bring out the best in each other and make a festive treat for the spring Jewish holiday of Shavuot, which commemorates the receipt of the Torah and is often celebrated with dairy foods.

Vigorously stir together the mascarpone, honey, and nutmeg to incorporate and lighten the cheese. If the strawberries are especially tart, you can add a little more honey to the filling. Refrigerate until ready to use (up to a day in advance). If the mixture seems too thick, stir in a little milk or light cream.

Wash and hull the berries; drain cut side down on a paper towel. Use a knife or small spoon to fill the hull completely with the cheese mixture.

Spread the cashews on a plate and gently press each berry, cheese side down, onto the cashews to cover the cheese. Serve immediately.

Yield: 12 to 24 stuffed berries (Dairy)

Note: *Look for mascarpone that is thick like cream cheese, such as Bel Gioioso brand. You can use cream cheese or light cream cheese if you can't find mascarpone; it's a different flavor, but equally good.*

1⅓ cups walnut pieces or halves

4 ready-to-bake sheets puff pastry (such as 2 boxes Pepperidge Farm brand, which is certified kosher pareve)

2 slices good-quality nondairy white or soft wheat sandwich bread, crusts removed and discarded

1 cup water

2 cloves garlic, peeled and sliced

⅛ teaspoon (generous) kosher salt, plus more, when frying, to taste

Freshly ground black pepper

Pinch of ground red (cayenne) pepper

Extra-virgin olive oil

1 pound ground chicken

3 tablespoons finely chopped shallots

Cooking spray

Walnut Chicken Piroshkis

Piroshkis are savory pastries from Russia's Jews. For an updated Jewish-Italian version, I combined lean ground chicken with nondairy Italian walnut sauce that gives a creamy texture and a garlicky, slightly nutty flavor. Of the two most common piroshki dough options, I favor pastry dough over yeast dough for its light and flaky quality (it's also the dough usually used in similar pastries called bourekas that are quite popular in Israel). Final plus: you can make these ahead and freeze—and then bake them straight from the freezer later.

Toast the walnuts by spreading on a baking pan and baking in a 350-degree oven, jostling the pan every few minutes, until lightly browned, 6 to 8 minutes.

Start 2 sheets of puff pastry thawing according to the package directions; start next 2 sheets about 15 minutes later.

Finely chop (by hand or in small food processor) ⅓ cup of the walnuts and set aside for the topping.

Tear the bread into chunks and place in a small bowl with 1 cup of water. Mash with the back of a fork until loosely combined. Process the bread mixture, remaining 1 cup of walnuts, garlic, ⅛ teaspoon salt, freshly ground black pepper to taste, and red pepper in a blender. Set aside.

Heat a thin layer of olive oil in a large nonstick skillet over medium-high heat. Add the ground chicken to the pan and break into small pieces. Season lightly with salt and black pepper. Cook 5 to 7 minutes, until lightly browned. Remove and set aside.

Add another light coat of olive oil to the skillet, and add the shallots and sauté until just softened, 1 to 2 minutes. Remove the pan from heat and add the walnut sauce. Reduce heat slightly, return pan to heat and stir until the sauce is thickened and vigorously bubbling, 1 to 2 minutes. Stir in ground chicken to coat. Remove from heat and let cool slightly.

Preheat the oven to 400 degrees. Line 2 baking sheets with parchment paper.

To make the pastries, blot dry 1 sheet of dough and unfold on a lightly floured surface. Gently roll to a 14-by-10-inch rectangle (less than 1/8-inch thick). Cut into approximate 3½-inch squares (see note). Place a scant 1 tablespoon of filling in the middle of a square and fold dough over to form a triangle. Pinch ends firmly to seal, and transfer to prepared baking sheet. Repeat with remaining dough. Spray tops of piroshkis lightly with cooking spray and sprinkle with reserved chopped walnuts. (Pastries can be frozen at this point.)

Bake for 14 to 16 minutes (adding about 4 minutes if frozen), rotating pans once, until golden brown. Remove to a wire rack to cool slightly before serving. (Alternatively, you can bake the first half of the batch while you prepare the second half.)

Yield: About 48 pastries (Meat)

Note: The seams of Pepperidge Farm sheets are 3½ inches apart; for the squares, orient the dough vertically and roll from middle up and from middle down. Then cut vertically along the 3 seams, and divide horizontally into 4 equal rows.

Chapter 6

Vegetables and Salads

Fresh ingredients, especially vegetables, are the signatures of Italian and Mediterranean cooking. Some vegetables that cross Italian and Jewish lines frequently are tomatoes, eggplants, artichokes, potatoes, and bell peppers, and boy, I love playing with all these. In this chapter, Tuscan Bread Salad employs fresh tomatoes and leftover bread to great effect; the Mediterranean dish Swiss Chard and Chickpeas combines fresh greens and beans. I reworked Eggplant Parmigiana with a very special red wine tomato sauce and created a creamy root vegetable dish. And I couldn't resist including mashed potatoes because they go so very well with so many things.

Reflections
ROOTS

Recipes
ROOT VEGETABLES
WITH BLUE CHEESE

GRILLED EGGPLANT
PARMIGIANA WITH RED WINE
MARINARA SAUCE

SPRING PEAS WITH
BUTTERED ALMONDS

SPICY SWEET PEPPER SALAD

SWISS CHARD AND CHICKPEAS

ZUCCHINI AND CORN WITH DILL

ROASTED ASPARAGUS

THE MASHED POTATO VARIATIONS

GRILLED VEGETABLES

BABY ARTICHOKES WITH
SAGE AND WHITE WINE

TUSCAN BREAD AND TOMATO SALAD

Roots

After just recently becoming Jewish, I landed in Israel with my soon-to-be husband Daryl, looking forward to meeting his family there and learning about the country, but not at all prepared for what befell me. Right after we arrived at our family's house in Haifa, I came down with "traveler's sickness."

Instead of taking us sightseeing, every member of the family joined the effort to revive me. They drove to the pharmacy for remedies. They joked to make me laugh. But nothing was working, and I retreated to bed. A few hours later, an aroma wafted in from the kitchen, and it smelled good. When I came downstairs, the family matriarch Malka gave me a warm, knowing smile. She ladled some golden broth into a wide shallow bowl and spooned in strands of egg noodles. After just a couple of sips of her homemade chicken soup, energy flowed to my tired limbs and the fog in my brain started to lift. It was the best meal I had in Israel, and the best example of the chicken soup cure I've ever known.

I might have been surprised at the family's good-natured effort to help me get better, especially since they had met me for the first time when I arrived in Tel Aviv. However, they were no ordinary family. Malka was the daughter of Clara, the teacher who helped Daryl's grandparents, father David, and uncle Henry survive the Holocaust. I had never met Clara, but I knew her story. Right then, through the kindness of her daughter Malka, I believed very much that I knew a little of her spirit, too.

We began our sightseeing. The family showed us as much of northern Israel as they could, from where the Scud missile landed in their backyard during the first Persian Gulf War to where Malka's husband, Dov, used to patrol the Lebanese border when he was in the Army. When their van got a flat tire, they changed to a doughnut spare tire and just kept driving (into the mountains no less!) and joking around. I admired the perseverance and humor they applied to almost every endeavor.

When we left Malka's family, we traveled by bus southeast and over the mountains into Jerusalem. The next morning, we went to the Western Wall, all that remains of the temple that was once central to Jewish life.

It would be entirely possible to see the Western Wall as a sorrowful place. But to me it wasn't. On the morning we visited, the ruins teemed with life—a bar mitzvah, people lost in silent and vocal prayers, and guards and tourists. Jewish and non-Jewish visitors alike could insert into the wall small prayers or notes—whatever was meaningful. Men and women had separate sections of the wall, so Daryl and I joined our respective lines. I carried a note on a small piece of paper folded over and over again so that it would fit into a crevice and stay there. As I got closer, I saw all the notes from the people before me, dotting the wall section within reach of human hands. I wondered what was on all those notes. What do people ask or say when they get this chance? I pushed my note into a little space.

Before we left Israel, there was one more stop. Upon arriving, I stepped out of the car, pausing to remove first one shoe and then the other, clasping them together in one hand as I walked across the sand toward the edge of the Mediterranean Sea, the body of water that touches both Israel and Italy. A low wave flattened and reached for me. I leaned over and lifted a palmful of seawater. Pleased to meet you, finally. The water slipped through my fingers, and back out to sea where it would touch other shores, including Italy's.

***

Ten years later, I reached Italy's shores myself. Setting foot in the old country of my dad's grandparents, across the Mediterranean from Israel, had long been

a goal. Here, though, my roots eluded me—I knew no connections to any possible relatives. My search instead focused on discovering a sense of the place and the culture of previous generations of my family. What might their lives have been like? How did they look? Maybe like that slight woman over there with dark wavy hair? And did that man just smile like my dad used to? Sometimes strangers would catch my gaze, and I'd wonder whether they could tell what I was looking for.

Seeing Italy also meant absorbing its history. And that's where the real surprise came. After visiting the Roman Coliseum, we stopped to see the Arch of Titus, a gray-brown stone structure, and came face-to-face with a striking scene—Roman soldiers attacking Jerusalem and carrying off a Jewish Torah scroll. The reenacted scene commemorates Rome's sacking of the city by future Emperor Titus in 70 C.E., when Roman forces destroyed Jerusalem's ancient temple and left only its Western Wall standing—that monument across the sea where we had stood equally amazed a decade ago. During their reign, the Romans also dispersed Jews from their homeland. This created the Jewish Diaspora, sending Jews all over the world, including Eastern Europe, where Daryl's grandparents would eventually live, and even Italy, where a small but vibrant Jewish-Italian community mostly thrived until World War II.

Italy's intense autumn sun sent a bead of sweat down my back. Seeing the arch put my search for all things Italian into the wider context of appreciating how Italian and Jewish roots intersected. It made more vivid and poignant the traces of Jewish life still to be found in Italy—like a restaurant dish of artichokes "in the Jewish style," a Moorish-style old synagogue in Florence, and the remains of a Jewish ghetto in Venice.

Who knows what Titus would think if he could see that Western Wall today, in the state of Israel. Rather than a sad ruin, it stands as a monument of survival—of people yearning and striving to hold on to their roots and seek a spiritual connection. There it endures, dotted with the hopes and prayers of thousands—including me, the Jewish and Italian woman on a cultural journey crisscrossing through history and geography.

2 tablespoons unsalted butter, divided

1 medium sweet onion, finely chopped

Salt and freshly ground black pepper

1 medium fennel bulb (about 1 pound), coarsely chopped, with 1 stalk reserved

2 medium to large Russet potatoes (about 1 pound), peeled and cut into matchstick strips (about 1½ to 2 inches long and about ¼ inch in diameter)

2 or 3 medium turnips (about ¾ pound), peeled and cut into matchsticks

¾ cup heavy cream

½ cup water

1 bay leaf, slightly crumpled

½ cup panko (Japanese breadcrumbs)

2 tablespoons finely chopped fresh chives

¼ to ⅓ pound blue cheese (preferably mild), cut into small pieces (see note)

Root Vegetables with Blue Cheese

Small bites of root vegetables popular in both Jewish and Italian dishes lend complementary mild and sweet flavors to this gratin. Dotted with blue cheese (see note) and finished with a crunchy herb topping, it showcases how layers of mild flavors can build up to something fantastic and comforting. Julienning the vegetables ensures the flavors blend and speeds the cooking.

Preheat the oven to 350 degrees. Use about ½ tablespoon of the butter to coat a 2-quart shallow casserole dish or similar (such as an 11-by-7-inch glass baking dish) and set aside.

Melt 1 tablespoon of butter in a large nonstick skillet over medium-high heat. Add the onion, sprinkle with salt and pepper, and cook, stirring frequently, until softened, 2 to 5 minutes. Melt in another ½ tablespoon of butter. Stir in the potatoes, fennel, and turnips. Stir constantly for 1 minute, then reduce heat slightly and cover pan. Stir about once a minute for 4 to 6 minutes, until vegetables soften slightly.

Combine the cream and water and add to the pan with the bay leaf. Remove and discard the fronds from the reserved fennel stalk and split the stalk in half lengthwise; add to the pan. Stir in ¼ teaspoon salt and black pepper to taste. Increase heat slightly and simmer for 3 more minutes, stirring occasionally. Discard bay leaf and fennel stalk.

Transfer vegetable mixture to the buttered baking dish. Bake for 30 to 40 minutes until vegetables are fork tender and tops are just starting to brown (mixture will be bubbly).

Combine the panko and chives. Remove the dish from the oven and nestle pieces of cheese evenly among the vegetables. Sprinkle with the panko and chives. Bake for 8 more minutes, then broil for 2 to 3 minutes until topping is golden brown. Let rest about 15 minutes before serving.

Yield: About 6 side-dish servings (Dairy)

Note: If you are not observing kosher rules, Gorgonzola dolce—a softer, milder form of the Italian blue cheese—makes this dish spectacular (however, this cheese does not seem to be currently available kosher certified).

Ingredients

*Red Wine Marinara Sauce
(makes about 3¼ cups)*
Extra-virgin olive oil

1 large sweet onion, chopped

Freshly ground black pepper

3 garlic cloves, minced

1 cup dry red wine

1 can (28 ounces) whole tomatoes, crushed with the back of a fork or cut up with kitchen shears

½ teaspoon dried thyme

⅛ teaspoon dried oregano

Kosher salt

Eggplant
3 medium eggplant, sliced into ½-inch-thick rounds

Extra-virgin olive oil

Kosher salt and freshly ground black pepper

2½ cups (about ¾ pound) shredded mozzarella cheese

½ cup fresh basil leaves, torn in half

Red wine tomato sauce

½ cup freshly grated Parmesan cheese

½ cup dried bread crumbs (such as panko) (optional)

Grilled Eggplant Parmigiana with Red Wine Marinara Sauce

Red wine and tomatoes combine for a mildly fruity, deep-red sauce that almost steals the show from the smoky grilled eggplant. Almost. With dramatic flavors, this is a slightly healthier version of an Italian classic, inspired by my mother-in-law Gloria's eggplant grilling method. The sauce and eggplant (technically a fruit) can be prepared ahead, then assembled and baked just before serving.

For the Sauce

Heat a thin coating of olive oil in large deep-sided pan (such as a Dutch oven) over medium heat. Add the onion, sprinkle lightly with freshly ground black pepper, and stir frequently until softened, 5 to 10 minutes. Add the garlic and cook, stirring constantly, 1 minute more. Increase the heat to medium-high, and stir in the wine and ½ cup of water. Boil to reduce the liquid by about half, 8 to 12 minutes. Stir in the tomatoes, thyme, and oregano. Simmer 20 to 30 minutes, stirring occasionally. Taste and add kosher salt and pepper if needed.

For the Eggplant

Preheat the grill. Toss the eggplant slices with olive oil to coat. Place on grill and season lightly with salt and freshly ground black pepper. Grill over medium-high heat, 2 to 4 minutes per side, until lightly browned. Remove and place on paper towels to drain. (Can be refrigerated for a few hours until ready to assemble dish.)

Preheat oven to 375 degrees.

Lightly coat the bottom of a 9-by-13-inch baking dish with olive oil. Place half the eggplant slices on the bottom, top with half the mozzarella, and place one piece of basil on top of each eggplant slice. Top with a layer of sauce. Repeat. Sprinkle the Parmesan cheese and bread crumbs over the top. Bake uncovered for 30 minutes, then broil for 1 to 2 minutes to brown the top. Serve warm.

Yield: 6 to 8 servings (Dairy)

Spring Peas with Buttered Almonds

1½ tablespoons plus ½ tablespoon unsalted butter

½ cup chopped blanched slivered almonds

Kosher salt

½ tablespoon extra-virgin olive oil

¾ cup finely chopped sweet onion (about half a medium-to-large onion)

2 garlic cloves, pressed through a garlic press or minced

3½ cups shelled fresh green peas

¾ cup vegetable broth, plus more if needed

1 teaspoon sugar

A traditional Florentine preparation of spring's fresh peas features prosciutto. But crispy, buttery almonds (a pleasure in their own right) offer an equally nice flavor and textural accent to the delicate green legumes.

Melt 1½ tablespoons of butter in a small saucepan over medium heat. When the butter begins to clear, add the almonds and cook, stirring every 10 to 15 seconds or so, until just starting to brown, 3 to 8 minutes. Remove from heat, stir a few more times, and set aside.

Warm the oil and ½ tablespoon of butter in a large nonstick skillet over medium-high heat and swirl to combine. Add the onion and sprinkle with kosher salt; cook, stirring constantly, for 2 minutes or until tender. Add the garlic, and cook, stirring, for about 30 seconds. Continuing to stir, add the peas and cook another 30 seconds. Stir in the broth and sugar. Bring to simmer and cover loosely. Cook for 20 to 25 minutes, until peas are tender (adding more broth if mixture dries out). Remove from heat and stir in almonds. Taste and add salt as needed. Serve warm or room temperature.

Yield: About 3 cups, 4 to 5 side-dish servings (Dairy)

Spicy Sweet Pepper Salad

Extra-virgin olive oil

5 bell peppers (preferably a combination of red, yellow, and orange), sliced into large cubes

1 red onion, chopped

2 garlic cloves, pressed through a garlic press or minced

¼ teaspoon crushed red pepper flakes, or to taste

1 can (14½ ounces) diced tomatoes

1 tablespoon red wine vinegar

Salt and freshly ground black pepper

2 tablespoons chopped fresh basil

Braised sweet bell peppers and tomatoes spiked with hot red pepper flakes bring on vibrant color and flavor in this side dish with roots in southern Italian cuisine and echoes of a Jewish-Moroccan pepper dish.

Heat a thin layer of oil in a large nonstick skillet or Dutch oven over medium-high heat. Add the peppers and onion. Cook, stirring frequently, until vegetables just begin to soften, 6 to 10 minutes.

Add the garlic and red pepper flakes, and cook, stirring constantly, for about 30 seconds. Stir in the tomatoes. Cover and simmer over medium-low heat for about 30 minutes, stirring occasionally. Add the vinegar, salt and pepper to taste, and basil and cook 5 more minutes, uncovered. Serve warm or at room temperature. Can be stored several days in the refrigerator. Bring to room temperature before serving.

Yield: About 5 cups (Pareve)

Swiss Chard and Chickpeas

Extra-virgin olive oil

1 large onion, finely chopped (about 1½ cups)

Salt and freshly ground black pepper

3 large garlic cloves, slivered

⅛ teaspoon crushed red pepper flakes

2 large bunches of red Swiss chard (1½ to 2 pounds total), rinsed well with stems and ribs removed and discarded, and with the leaves coarsely chopped

1 cup seeded and diced Roma (plum) tomatoes

1 can (16 ounces) chickpeas, well rinsed and drained

1 cup chicken or vegetable broth

½ cup water

¼ large lemon or ½ small lemon

Dishes featuring wilted greens and beans are typical of the Mediterranean, and a Jewish-Syrian recipe specifically combines chard and chickpeas—and I can see why. Swiss chard is sturdier than spinach but still mild, a good partner for toothsome chickpeas. With the addition of some crushed red pepper and tomatoes, this dish bubbles its way to a nuanced earthy flavor, brightened with a last-minute squeeze of lemon.

Warm a thin (quarter-inch or so) layer of olive oil in a large deep-sided pan (preferably a Dutch oven) over medium-high heat. Add the onion and sprinkle with salt and pepper. Cook, stirring frequently, until the onion softens, 3 to 5 minutes. Add the garlic and red pepper flakes, and cook, stirring, 1 to 2 minutes until the garlic becomes fragrant but not brown.

Add about half the chard to the pan, turning with a spatula. As soon as it begins to wilt (and makes room), stir in the remaining chard plus the tomatoes, chickpeas, broth, water, and ¼ teaspoon salt. Reduce heat to medium and cover. Cook, stirring occasionally, until greens are just tender, 15 to 20 minutes. Remove lid, increase heat to medium-high, and boil until most of the liquid evaporates, 8 to 12 more minutes.

To serve, transfer to a platter or wide bowl and squeeze juice from lemon over top.

Yield: 3 to 4 cups, or 4 to 6 side-dish servings (Meat with chicken broth; Pareve with vegetable broth)

3 medium zucchini, ends removed

1½ teaspoons kosher salt, plus more to taste

1 tablespoon plus 2 teaspoons extra-virgin olive oil

2 tablespoons plus 1 tablespoon unsalted butter or margarine

1 medium sweet onion, chopped

3 medium ears of corn, kernels removed from the cob (about 2 generous cups)

3 tablespoons chopped fresh dill

Freshly ground black pepper

Zucchini and Corn with Dill

Fresh zucchini (and even the blossom, stuffed with cheese and fried) is very popular in Italian cooking. For this side dish, I combine zucchini and corn with one of my favorite herbs, dill— often associated with Jewish dishes. When fresh corn isn't available, substitute an equal amount of thawed frozen corn.

Cut the zucchini crosswise into 2 or 3 pieces. Grate longwise across the large holes of a box grater, stopping before reaching the seeds and core, which should be discarded. Place grated zucchini in a large colander set over a medium bowl or in the sink. Toss with 1½ teaspoons of kosher salt. Let drain for 5 to 10 minutes. Press zucchini with paper towels or a kitchen towel to remove as much liquid as possible. Toss with 2 teaspoons of olive oil.

Melt 2 tablespoons of the butter in a large nonstick skillet over medium-high heat. Add 1 tablespoon of olive oil and the onion, and cook, stirring frequently, for 3 to 4 minutes, until the onion begins to soften. Add the zucchini and corn and stir to combine; break up zucchini clumps with tongs or a fork if needed. Cook, turning mixture every couple of minutes, until corn is tender, about 8 minutes. Off heat, stir in remaining tablespoon of butter (cut into 3 or 4 pieces), the dill, and salt and pepper to taste. Serve warm.

Yield: 3½ to 4 cups (4 to 5 side dish servings) (Dairy with butter; Pareve with margarine)

1 bunch (about 1½ pounds) asparagus, rinsed with tough ends removed

Extra-virgin olive oil

Kosher salt

Freshly ground black pepper

Garlic powder

Roasted Asparagus

Roasting is a no-fuss way to bring out lightly caramelized flavor in asparagus, and I never tire of the way it tastes or the way it works with so many dishes.

Preheat the oven to 400 degrees.

Place asparagus in a bowl or resealable plastic bag and toss with enough olive oil and seasonings to coat. Spread spears in a single layer on a large baking sheet. Bake until just tender, 10 to 15 minutes, and then broil for 1 to 3 minutes to brown the tops a bit more. Remove and serve warm or at room temperature.

Yield: 4 to 6 side-dish servings (Pareve)

6 pounds russet potatoes, peeled and quartered

Salt

1 cup milk, plus more if needed

8 tablespoons (1 stick) unsalted butter or margarine, cut into 4 or 5 pieces

Freshly ground black pepper

1 cup light or regular coconut milk plus more as needed (for nondairy version only)

The Mashed Potato Variations

It helps to have a few tricks up your sleeve for mashed potatoes, a favorite side dish. The classic version with butter and milk never fails to please, and the nondairy version can take a seat next to any meat entrée. Finally, a make-ahead technique takes the pressure off bringing a big meal to the table. Although it takes an extra couple of minutes, using a potato ricer turns out nice fluffy potatoes. This makes a big batch.

Cook potatoes with 2 teaspoons salt at a low boil until tender when pierced with a fork, about 20 minutes.

Drain water from pan, and then return pan to heat for 1 to 2 minutes, stirring constantly, to remove any leftover moisture.

Separately, heat the milk until hot but not simmering.

Rice or mash the potatoes. Stir in the butter and salt and pepper to taste. Gradually add the warm milk, stirring to incorporate, until potatoes are desired consistency.

Make-Ahead Mashed Potatoes
Follow recipe above. Transfer mashed potatoes to a double-boiler or a pot set over a second pot containing hot but not simmering water. Smooth to make an even layer. Cover the potatoes completely with a thin layer of hot milk. Cover and hold for up to 3 hours. Check periodically and add more milk if potatoes start to dry out. To serve, bring the water to simmer and heat the potatoes through. Beat to incorporate the milk layer, and add more milk if needed.

Nondairy (Pareve) Mashed Potatoes
In the traditional and make-ahead recipes above, substitute coconut milk for the milk (coconut milk gives the potatoes just a slight sweetness) and margarine for the butter. Proceed as directed.

Optional Stir-Ins
- A few cloves roasted or toasted garlic
- Ground red (cayenne) pepper, to taste
- Shredded sharp Cheddar cheese

Yield: About 11 cups (Dairy or Pareve)

Vegetables, washed, from among the following:

Asparagus spears, tough ends removed

Portobello mushroom caps

Roma (plum) tomatoes, sliced in half lengthwise

Red, green, and yellow bell peppers, quartered

Red onions, quartered

Zucchini, yellow squash, or eggplant, ends removed and sliced slightly diagonally

Scallions, cleaned and root end trimmed, half of green end removed

Dressing

Extra-virgin olive oil

Kosher salt

Freshly ground black pepper

Garlic powder (except on scallions)

Grilled Vegetables

Simply grilling vegetables often renders their flavor spectacular, and that's why I serve mixed grilled vegetables so often. They look beautiful arranged on a platter or tray, and they can also be made a little ahead and served at room temperature. Adjust seasonings to your tastes.

Preheat grill to medium-high.

Toss prepared vegetables in bowls or in large resealable bags (grouping by vegetable or pairing like vegetables, such as zucchini and yellow squash) with a generous coating of olive oil and spices to taste.

Vegetables can rest at room temperature for 20 minutes before grilling. Grill over medium-high heat. Turn once when just starting to brown, usually 3 to 4 minutes for more delicate vegetables and slices (like the asparagus and zucchini), and 6 to 8 minutes for thicker vegetables (such as the mushrooms).

Serve warm or at room temperature.

Yield: Varies (Pareve)

Variation: A sprinkling of toasted pine nuts and feta cheese (if not serving with meat) makes an attractive and flavorful garnish to the vegetable platter.

Juice of 1 lemon

12 baby artichokes

1 tablespoon plus 1 tablespoon unsalted butter

6 sage leaves

1 large garlic clove, slivered

Kosher salt and freshly ground black pepper

1 cup water

¼ cup dry white wine such as Pinot Grigio

¼ cup chopped salted pistachios for garnish (optional)

Baby Artichokes with Sage and White Wine

Besides being deliciously tender, baby artichokes offer a more manageable size and lack the fuzzy choke to remove, making them easier to prepare as a side dish vegetable. Just about all you need is a little sage, white wine, and butter—and for fun, some pistachios for garnish.

Add the lemon juice to a large bowl of cold water (enough liquid to cover the artichokes). Wash the artichokes, remove any tough outer leaves, and trim the stem and cut off the top third of the artichoke. Halve or quarter and drop into the lemon water (which reduces browning). Drain just before cooking.

Melt 1 tablespoon of butter in a deep-sided pan with a lid (such as a Dutch oven) over medium heat. Add the sage leaves, and stir for 1 minute until they are fragrant and starting to wilt. Add the garlic, increase the heat slightly, and sauté for about 1 minute, until the garlic is fragrant. Add the drained artichokes, sprinkle with salt and pepper, and sauté for 1 to 2 minutes. Stir in 1 cup of water and ¼ cup white wine. Bring to a boil, and then lower to a simmer. Cover and cook until the artichokes are tender, about 20 minutes.

Remove the artichokes. Cut the remaining tablespoon of butter in small pieces and toss with the artichokes until melted and well combined. Top with a sprinkling of pepper and, if using, chopped pistachios.

Yield: 4 to 6 side-dish servings (Dairy)

Tuscan Bread and Tomato Salad

1 large loaf of 1- or 2-day-old Italian or country-style bread

$1/4$ cup water

$1/3$ cup red wine vinegar

$1^1/_2$ pounds ripe tomatoes, cut into cubes (approximately 3 cups)

1 medium red onion, thinly sliced and rings separated

Kosher salt and freshly ground black pepper

$1/3$ cup extra-virgin olive oil

$1/3$ cup fresh basil leaves, chopped

When no one is looking, I sometimes use my bread to lift from my plate every last bit of tomato sauce or tomato, mozzarella, and basil salad. This simple Tuscan salad is what happens when you skip all pretenses and throw the bread and tomatoes together at the outset. It's also an ingenious way to use a day-old loaf and summer's ripest fruit for a very fresh dish. The salad can be assembled a few hours ahead and left at room temperature. If you have only fresh bread, lightly toast it before using so that it can hold its own.

Remove the crusts from the bread and tear or cut it into approximately $1/2$- to 1-inch cubes. Place in a large bowl, and sprinkle with the water and vinegar. Add tomatoes and onions, and sprinkle lightly with salt and pepper. Add olive oil, a few tablespoons at a time, until the salad is well dressed but not weighted down. Let stand at room temperature for 30 minutes (or up to 6 hours), taste and adjust seasonings if needed, and toss in basil just before serving.

Yield: Approximately 6 side-dish servings (Pareve)

Chapter 7

Eggs and Cheese

Eggs and cheese play essential roles in many recipes, those from breakfast to dessert. Eggs offer great nutrition—protein, vitamin A, calcium, magnesium, and iron—as well as versatility. The classic Israeli breakfast features hardboiled eggs, so I created a version of stuffed eggs with smoked salmon and Italian cheese. Cheeses found commonly in Jewish cooking include cream cheese, which I use in my favorite rugelach recipe here, and farmer's cheese, for which I substituted Italian ricotta in the creamy cheese blintz recipe. Italian fontina goes especially well in egg dishes like the butternut squash tart and the asparagus frittata, and mascarpone and challah create a decadent bread pudding. Some of my most pleasant recipe development surprises occurred while creating this chapter—the Mediterranean eggs poached in tomato sauce make for a hearty, sensational-tasting breakfast, while lemon-ricotta pancakes turn out beautiful and luscious—everything a good cheese and cream recipe should be.

The Missing Ingredient

With becoming Jewish has come some new traditions. One is celebrating Hanukkah in December. I like that holiday. It doesn't require fasting or eating matzah—two very good things. Also, it's quiet and peaceful. With an additional candle lit each evening, by the seventh and eighth days, the menorah brightens the whole living room, triumphing over the dark December night, even if only for an hour. But after my first year, I knew something was missing. And it wasn't a Christmas tree.

It was the aromas of brown sugar, cinnamon, vanilla, butter, and chocolate hanging about the house—the scents I looked forward to every December for as long as I could remember. That's when my mom baked cookies, dozens of them, following the traditions of her mother and grandmother. My brother Brian and I

"helped," though when we were smaller, that usually involved making more messes than our help was worth, and standing over the baking sheet just pulled from the oven to bite into chocolate chip cookies and lick the bits of chocolate melting out from the inside.

We also made hard candy for many years. In a small saucepan, my mom would boil sugar, corn syrup, and water until the mixture reached the "hard crack" notch on her candy thermometer inserted in the liquid. Then she'd stir in the flavoring and the color, creating a cloud of intensely fragrant steam. She would dash across the kitchen and pour the molten concoction onto a buttered marble slab, where it would spread out like a stained glass pancake. It would immediately start to harden, and the race was on. We'd start cutting the sticky mass with buttered scissors to create bite-size pieces. In another 60 seconds, the candy would be too hard to cut.

When all the flavors were boiled, cut, and cooled, they all went into a big jar or clear bag to be thoroughly mixed into a kaleidoscope of colorful bites. Then we'd place handfuls into individual bags held closed with a thin piece of curled ribbon to give away. I always looked forward to that part the most. Hardly anyone I knew had ever tasted homemade rock candy before or received it as a gift. As our candy tradition continued over the years, friends sometimes said, "I've been waiting for this all year!" Sometimes they told us what flavors their families liked the best, and I liked knowing that giving the sweets passed on not only the pleasure of eating but also the pleasure of sharing. Like little rocks splashing and creating ripples in the pool of good will.

When Hanukkah became part of my year, I found myself unsure of what to do. The different holiday had different meaning as well as new gifts and foods that I loved, like the latkes, little patties of fried potato perfection. Nonetheless, my oven seemed especially cold and the celebration felt a little empty. I missed walking in the footsteps of my maternal lineage, and even more, I missed creating something delicious to give away.

Coming across Hanukkah cookie cutters at the store motivated me to revisit the baking tradition that seemed to be the missing ingredient in my Hanukkah celebration. I returned to the kitchen with my old sugar cookie recipe to cream butter and sugar, fire up the oven, and roll dough on a countertop dusted lightly with flour. I cut out shapes of dreidels and menorahs and sprinkled them with blue-colored sugar. After baking, these tender buttery cookies had cuteness going for them but couldn't overcome my nagging feeling that they were merely the Hanukkah bush of Christmas cookies. The search continued.

It took me to recipes for the little Jewish pastries called rugelach, sometimes made at Hanukkah. They fit the holiday much better, especially with a cream-cheese dough that matches Hanukkah's other food theme, dairy foods. Rugelach though, like hard candy, involved some potchke (fussiness) as my mother-in-law would say, with creaming, rolling, chilling, more rolling, and baking to just the right moment. Plus the bland, dry ones I tried from the store made me fear that the cookies wouldn't be worth the effort. But a recipe for a cinnamon pecan version and another using Italian hazelnut paste intrigued me enough to get me to face the mixing bowl.

After following all the steps and feeling relieved that at least they looked like rugelach, I slid two pans of pastries in the oven. And in the warm oasis of the kitchen, I savored the scents of butter and cinnamon and peeked through the oven window, watching my little crescents start to expand, then glisten and brown.

Once my pans came out of the oven, I reviewed my work, which involved tasting, of course. Choosing the most misshapen of each kind, I tried my first homemade Jewish pastries for Hanukkah. And with just one bite, I could tell that the slightly firm but delicate little cookies were decadent and worth every calorie. From the cinnamon batch, the apricot filling had melted out, forming an almost candy-like crust on the bottom of the cooling pastries. They were unlike any Christmas cookie—or any other cookie—I had ever had.

I gave away several small boxes of rugelach. And saw smiles and glowing faces when people tried them. And the next year, when I made them to give away again, one of the recipients said, "I've been waiting for these all year!"

Cream Cheese Rugelach with Cinnamon and Brown Sugar

1 package (8 ounces) cream cheese, softened

1/2 pound (2 sticks) unsalted butter, softened

1/4 cup plus 6 tablespoons granulated sugar

1/8 teaspoon salt

1 1/2 teaspoons vanilla

2 1/4 cups all-purpose flour

1/4 cup firmly packed light brown sugar

3/4 teaspoon ground cinnamon

1 cup pecans, finely chopped

1/2 cup apricot preserves at room temperature

1 egg lightly beaten with 1 tablespoon milk

Topping
1 1/2 tablespoons granulated sugar

1/2 teaspoon ground cinnamon

The high regard for rugelach appears right in the name—it likely comes from the Yiddish word for royal. Every year I make dozens of this version of the tender Jewish pastry, with the homey flavors of cinnamon, pecans, and a kiss of apricot. These also can be made in advance (see note).

Cream the cheese and butter in a large bowl until smooth and light. Add 1/4 cup granulated sugar, salt, and vanilla. Stir in the flour until just combined. The dough will be very sticky. Add a little additional flour if needed to make it cohesive.

Divide it into 4 equal pieces and roll each piece into a ball. Place 1 ball on a large piece of plastic wrap, gently press into a disk shape, and then enclose in the plastic. Repeat with the other 3 balls. Refrigerate for 1 hour or freeze for 20 minutes.

Make the filling by combining 6 tablespoons of granulated sugar, the brown sugar, 3/4 teaspoon cinnamon, and the pecans. Line a large baking sheet with parchment paper and set aside.

Remove 1 disk from the refrigerator; unwrap and place dough on a floured surface. Gently roll into an approximate 9-inch circle. Spread a generous 1/2 tablespoon of the apricot preserves over the dough to about 1/4 inch from the edge. Sprinkle evenly with a scant 1/2 cup of brown sugar filling and gently press. Cut the circle into 12 wedges. Starting at the wide edge, roll up each triangle. Place the formed pastries seam side down on the prepared baking sheet. Refrigerate for about 20 minutes or freeze for about 10 minutes. Repeat with remaining dough.

Preheat the oven to 350 degrees.

Make the topping by combining the 1 1/2 tablespoons sugar and the 1/2 teaspoon cinnamon.

Brush each pastry with the egg and milk mixture, and sprinkle lightly with sugar-cinnamon topping. Bake for 25 to 35 minutes, until well browned. Remove from oven, and let rest on the cookie sheet for 2 to 3 minutes before transferring rugelach to a wire rack. Cool completely before storing in an airtight container.

Yield: 48 rugelach (Dairy)

Note: Assembled pastries can be frozen and baked at a later time. Defrost partially before placing in oven, and allow extra time for baking.

Extra-virgin olive oil

1 red bell pepper, coarsely
chopped

Kosher salt and freshly ground
black pepper

1 garlic clove, minced

¼ teaspoon crushed red pepper
flakes

2 cans (14½ ounces each) diced
tomatoes (preferably fire roasted)

1 can (14 ounces) artichoke
hearts, drained and quartered

1 tablespoon chopped Italian
(flat-leaf) parsley, plus additional
for garnish

6 large eggs

12 thick slices of Italian bread

½ cup grated mozzarella cheese

¼ cup chopped pitted Kalamata
olives (optional)

1 cup ricotta cheese (mixed with
1 tablespoon milk if dry)

Mediterranean Eggs with Tomatoes and Artichokes

Eggs become an extraordinary dish when nestled to cook in a Mediterranean tomato and vegetable sauce and served together with creamy cheese and chewy bread—an idea you'll find variations of in Jewish-Italian (uova al pomodoro, eggs with tomatoes) and Israeli (shakshuka, or all mixed up) recipe collections. This recipe poaches the eggs but scrambling is also an option (see note).

Heat a thin layer of olive oil in a large nonstick skillet over medium-high heat. Add the chopped red pepper, season lightly with salt and pepper, and cook, stirring frequently, for 3 to 5 minutes, until starting to soften. Add the garlic and red pepper flakes and sauté 1 minute. Reduce heat to medium, stir in tomatoes, artichokes, and 1 tablespoon of parsley. Cook 6 to 10 minutes, until sauce thickens slightly. Form 6 wells with the back of a spoon.

Break one egg into each of the 6 wells, and sprinkle lightly with salt and pepper. Cover the pan loosely with foil and cook about 10 minutes, or until the eggs reach preferred doneness.

Meanwhile, toast the bread. Prepare 6 individual plates with two pieces of toast each. Top toast with one egg and a spoonful of the tomato mixture. Sprinkle with mozzarella, olives (if using), and parsley and top with a spoonful of ricotta. Serve warm.

Yield: 6 servings (Dairy)

Note: If you prefer scrambled eggs, before adding the eggs to the sauce, lightly beat them with 3 tablespoons milk and a sprinkling of salt and pepper. Divide the mixture among the 6 wells and proceed with the recipe. The scrambled eggs might seep a little bit from their wells, but they will cook and taste just fine.

Lemon-Ricotta Pancakes with Limoncello Cream

These luscious pancakes made with ricotta, a cheese of Italian origin, should be made ahead—really. Reheating in the oven mellows the cheese and lemon flavor and perfects the texture so that a slightly crispy exterior gives way to a creamy interior. I love serving these as a "sandwich" with cream spiked with limoncello, a lemon-flavored liqueur originating from the Amalfi Coast and Sicily. The short stack makes a beautiful and appetizing presentation—especially for dairy-focused celebrations such as Hanukkah or Shavuot.

Pancakes
1½ cups all-purpose flour

1 teaspoon baking powder

½ teaspoon baking soda

¼ teaspoon ground nutmeg

½ teaspoon salt

3 large eggs, separated

1½ cups buttermilk

1 cup whole-milk ricotta cheese

3 tablespoons sugar

1 teaspoon vanilla extract

2 tablespoons lemon zest (from 2 large lemons)

Cooking spray

Limoncello Cream
2 cups heavy whipping cream

½ teaspoon vanilla extract

3 tablespoons limoncello

1½ tablespoons sugar

Garnish
Fresh blueberries or other berries (optional)

Lightly whisk together the flour, baking powder, baking soda, nutmeg, and salt in a bowl or on a sheet of wax paper. In a large mixing bowl, whisk egg yolks, buttermilk, ricotta cheese, sugar, vanilla, and lemon zest. In a separate bowl, beat the egg whites until they hold stiff peaks.

Sprinkle the dry ingredients over the ricotta mixture and stir until just incorporated (will still be a bit lumpy). Fold in the egg whites until just a few stray streaks of white remain.

Heat a griddle to medium-high and spray with cooking spray. Drop ¼ cupfuls of batter onto griddle; spread gently with the back of a spoon to make an approximate 3½-inch circle. Cook until golden brown on both sides, and transfer to a wire rack to cool. Repeat with remaining batter.

When pancakes are completely cool, wrap and freeze.

To serve, preheat the oven to 375 degrees. Prepare two baking sheets, placing an ovenproof wire rack on each one. Place frozen pancakes in a single layer on the wire racks and bake until warmed and slightly crispy, rotating pans and turning pancakes halfway through, 16 to 22 minutes.

Meanwhile, combine the heavy cream, vanilla, and limoncello. Beat on high speed. As the cream gains a little volume, sprinkle sugar over, and continue beating until the cream holds soft peaks.

When pancakes are done, place a generous dollop of whipped cream between 2 pancakes and top with another spoonful of cream. Scatter fresh berries over top and sides. The cream will start to melt, which is lovely. Serve immediately.

Yield: 20 to 22 small pancakes, or 10 or 11 pancake sandwiches (1 to 2 sandwiches per serving) (Dairy)

1 unbaked piecrust for a double-crust pie (see note)

2½ cups peeled and cubed butternut squash

Extra-virgin olive oil

1 medium onion, finely chopped (about 1 cup)

7 large eggs

1⅓ cups milk

1 cup heavy cream

¾ teaspoon (generous) ground nutmeg

¼ teaspoon salt

Freshly ground black pepper

2 cups shredded fontina cheese

¼ cup freshly grated Parmesan cheese

Dash of ground red (cayenne) pepper (optional)

Butternut Squash Tart

Come fall and winter, this lightly textured egg tart graced with Italian fontina cheese and bites of butternut squash seems about perfect for a Rosh Hashanah or Sukkot gathering—or just about any brunch. You can make the dish ahead, refrigerate, and reheat at serving time.

Preheat the oven to 350 degrees.

Roll the dough to fit a 9-by-13- or a 9-by-12-inch baking dish or pan. Transfer the dough to the pan, and gently press to fit about ¾ of the way up the sides, trimming to even the edge.

Meanwhile, microwave the cubes with a little water in a covered dish until tender, about 4 minutes. Drain and let cool slightly.

Heat a thin layer of olive oil in a medium-sized nonstick skillet over medium heat. Add the onion and season with salt and pepper. Cook, stirring frequently, until softened and just starting to brown, 4 to 5 minutes. Set aside to cool slightly.

In a large bowl, lightly whisk the eggs, and then whisk in the milk, cream, nutmeg, salt, and pepper to taste.

Spread the squash cubes, onion, and fontina and Parmesan cheeses over the bottom of the piecrust. Pour the egg mixture over top and lightly dust with ground red pepper.

Bake for 50 to 60 minutes, until set and golden brown. Serve warm.

Yield: Approximately 12 servings (Dairy)

Note: If using store-bought pastry crusts, check the ingredients list (some contain lard, or rendered pork fat, which is not kosher).

Frittata with Asparagus, Leeks, and Fontina

1½ cups of ½-inch asparagus pieces (the tops and top halves of about 1 pound of thin spears)

1 thinly sliced and halved leek (the white part plus about an inch of the pale green part)

7 large eggs

Kosher salt

Freshly ground black pepper

Pinch of ground red (cayenne) pepper

⅔ cup shredded fontina cheese

½ cup freshly grated Parmesan cheese, with 1 tablespoon reserved

½ tablespoon unsalted butter

½ tablespoon extra-virgin olive oil

Mild, with a flavor that falls somewhere between garlic and onion, leeks (a favored vegetable in Jewish cuisine) add dimension to an Italian frittata studded with asparagus tips. You'll need an ovenproof skillet, preferably nonstick.

In the microwave, cook the asparagus pieces and leeks until asparagus is crisp-tender (2 to 3 minutes on high power). Drain.

In a medium bowl, lightly beat the eggs. Stir in the asparagus and leeks, salt and pepper to taste, cayenne pepper, fontina, and all but 1 tablespoon of the Parmesan cheese.

Preheat the broiler.

Heat the butter and oil in a large ovenproof skillet over medium-high heat, and swirl to coat the pan. Pour egg mixture into the skillet and lower the heat to medium. Cook without stirring, 10 to 14 minutes, until the bottom is set but the surface is still runny.

Wrap the skillet handle in foil to protect it and place the skillet under the broiler. Cook a few seconds until top just sets. The frittata should be firm but not dry. Remove immediately and sprinkle with reserved Parmesan cheese. Slide onto a plate, slice into wedges, and serve.

Yield: 6 to 8 servings (Dairy)

Pudding

9 loosely packed cups cubed challah bread from one 12-ounce loaf (cut into about ³/₄- to 1-inch cubes, crusts okay but discard thicker pieces)

Butter for coating the baking dish

1 cup firmly packed light brown sugar

1 teaspoon ground cinnamon

¹/₂ teaspoon salt

1 cup chopped dried apple

³/₄ cup chopped pecans

7 large egg yolks

2 cups heavy cream

1¹/₂ cups whole milk

4 tablespoons (¹/₂ stick) unsalted butter, melted and cooled slightly

3 teaspoons vanilla

¹/₂ cup mascarpone

Topping

2¹/₂ tablespoons light brown sugar

1 teaspoon ground cinnamon

¹/₄ cup chopped pecans

Garnish

8 ounces mascarpone

2 tablespoons honey (or more to taste)

Challah Bread Pudding with Apples and Mascarpone

This bread pudding features some of my favorite flavors—apples, cinnamon, brown sugar, pecans, and a little mascarpone—and the dense tender challah provides the perfect canvas. The topping of nuts and sugar offers a little crunch, and a final dollop of honey-sweetened mascarpone gives a contrasting cool creaminess. To prevent an overly "eggy" flavor, the recipe uses just egg yolks. Note that you'll need to chop 1 cup of pecans for the full recipe, and you'll need one and a half 8-ounce containers of mascarpone.

Preheat the oven to 325 degrees.

Spread the challah cubes in a single layer on a baking sheet, and toast, tossing occasionally, until just dry but not browned, 10 to 15 minutes. Remove and cool. Meanwhile, butter a 9-by-13-inch baking dish and set aside.

Combine the brown sugar, cinnamon, salt, apple, and ³/₄ cup chopped pecans in a medium bowl. In a large bowl, lightly whisk together the egg yolks, cream, milk, melted butter, and vanilla.

Add the challah cubes to the egg mixture, then gently stir in the brown sugar mixture. Transfer to the buttered baking dish and smooth out. Let stand 25 to 30 minutes, occasionally pressing the top cubes into the liquid. Right before baking, nestle teaspoonfuls of the ¹/₂ cup of mascarpone evenly over the casserole, and then lightly smear with a knife (no need to cover the whole casserole). Combine the topping ingredients (brown sugar, cinnamon, and the ¼ cup chopped pecans) and sprinkle over the casserole.

Bake for 30 to 40 minutes, until set (no liquid seeps when pudding is pressed in center) and reading at least 170 degrees on an instant-read thermometer. Remove to a wire rack and cool about 30 minutes before cutting into squares and serving. Combine the mascarpone and honey and place a spoonful on top of each portion. Refrigerate leftovers (it's good cold or can be reheated).

Yield: 8 to 12 servings (Dairy)

3 small red or yellow bell peppers, cut in half lengthwise and seeded and cored

Extra-virgin olive oil

3 small zucchini, cut in half lengthwise, ends trimmed, and pulp removed and discarded or saved for another use (the shells should be 1/4- to 1/3-inch thick)

2 cups low-moisture ricotta cheese

2 tablespoons heavy cream, plus more as needed

2 cups loosely packed fresh basil leaves, finely chopped

1 cup plus 1/3 cup freshly grated Parmesan cheese

2 small garlic cloves, pressed through a garlic press or minced

Squeeze of fresh lemon juice (about 1 teaspoon)

1/2 teaspoon salt

Freshly ground black pepper

Hot water (3 to 6 tablespoons) as needed

Ricotta-Stuffed Vegetables

Fresh peppers and zucchini overflow with a basil-spiked ricotta cheese filling lightly browned in the oven. So attractive on the plate and both light and filling. Serve as a side dish or vegetarian entrée.

Preheat the broiler. Place peppers skin-side up on a foil-lined baking pan and brush lightly with olive oil. Broil for 5 to 9 minutes, until the skins show just the first touch of brown. Remove from the oven and drain the peppers.

Preheat the oven to 450 degrees.

Coat 1 large baking dish (such as 15-by-10-inch) or 2 smaller dishes with olive oil or cooking spray. Arrange the zucchini shells and pepper halves in the dish, hollow sides up.

Thoroughly combine the ricotta and 2 tablespoons of the heavy cream, adding additional cream as needed to smooth out. Stir in the basil, 1 cup of Parmesan cheese, garlic, lemon juice, salt, and pepper to taste. If mixture is too thick, add hot water by the tablespoonful until smooth.

Press the filling lightly into the zucchini and pepper shells. Sprinkle with remaining 1/3 cup Parmesan cheese. Bake for 25 to 30 minutes until the filling is lightly browned. Serve warm.

Yield: 6 stuffed zucchini and 6 stuffed peppers (Dairy)

Grilled Mozzarella, Tomato, and Pesto Panini

4 Italian ciabatta rolls (or one loaf, cut into 4 or 5 pieces)

1 pound whole-milk, low-moisture mozzarella, sliced about ¼-inch thick

½ cup freshly grated Parmesan cheese

1 can (14 ounces) artichoke hearts, drained and chopped

2 medium tomatoes, sliced and drained of excess seeds and juice

Freshly ground black pepper

¼ to ⅓ cup basil pesto (see recipe on p. 37)

Extra-virgin olive oil

My childhood favorite grilled cheese with tomatoes goes Mediterranean here with mozzarella, tomatoes, pesto, and artichoke hearts. Besides nice flavor, the artichokes provide a meat-like texture among the tender tomatoes and creamy melted cheese, and the fresh pesto really hits the flavor out of the park. A large skillet and another heavy pan are all the equipment you really need, but if you've got a sandwich grill, use it (just follow your appliance's instructions).

Split the ciabatta rolls in half horizontally. On the bottom half, layer the mozzarella, Parmesan, artichoke hearts, tomatoes, black pepper, and pesto. Replace top of bread and press the sandwich together.

Heat a layer of olive oil in a large skillet over medium-high heat. Transfer the sandwich to the pan and top with another heavy pan. Grill for 2 to 4 minutes, until bottom is golden brown. Turn over, and grill the other side of the sandwich a few minutes until the bread is toasted and the cheese has melted.

Yield: 4 servings (Dairy)

Note: Whole-milk mozzarella melts more quickly, but part-skim works, too (it just might remain a little firmer).

Parmesan Crisps

1 cup finely shredded Parmigiano-Reggiano cheese (not grated to a powder; you need small shreds for a lattice effect)

2 teaspoons almond flour or finely ground almonds

Freshly ground black pepper (optional)

The virtues of Parmesan crisps are many—easy, fast, crispy, cheesy, OK for Passover, fun (almost addictive) to munch, beautiful as a garnish, gluten-free … I'll stop there. You just need good-quality Parmigiano-Reggiano cheese and some ground almonds. If they don't come out crispy (they will still taste good), bake them a minute or two longer the next time.

Preheat the oven to 350 degrees and line a baking sheet with parchment paper.

Use a fork to toss together the cheese and almond flour. Spoon heaping 1-tablespoon mounds on the baking sheet, and then lightly smooth to 3-inch circles (gently nudge cheese to close any gaps that form). If you like, sprinkle half the batch with black pepper for variety. Bake until lightly browned all over, 9 to 11 minutes.

Remove and wait 30 seconds. Use a metal spatula to loosen and transfer the crisps to a wire rack to cool completely. The crisps can be stored between layers of wax paper in an airtight container for a few days.

Yield: 10 to 11 Parmesan crisps (Dairy)

Filling

1 pound (about 2 cups) whole-milk ricotta cheese (drained if watery)

1/2 cup sour cream

1/2 cup mascarpone or cream cheese

1 tablespoon butter, melted

Pinch of salt

2 tablespoons sugar

1 teaspoon ground cinnamon

1 teaspoon grated orange zest

2 tablespoons fresh orange juice

1 teaspoon vanilla extract

2 tablespoons all-purpose flour (if needed)

Pancakes

1 1/2 cups whole or 2 percent milk

6 large eggs

1 1/2 cups all-purpose flour

1/2 teaspoon (scant) salt

Melted unsalted butter (about 3 tablespoons) for frying

Butter for coating the baking dish

Confectioner's sugar for garnish (optional)

Blueberry Sauce

3/4 cup of sugar, or more to taste

1 1/2 tablespoons cornstarch

3 cups fresh blueberries (or 3 cups frozen blueberries, not thawed)

3/4 cup of water

3 tablespoons freshly squeezed orange juice, or to taste

Topping

8 tablespoons (1 stick) unsalted butter, softened

1/4 cup light brown sugar

2 1/2 tablespoons cornstarch

Orange-Ricotta Blintzes with Blueberry Sauce

These thin, cheese-stuffed pancakes—similar to French crepes or Italian crespelle—are a Jewish specialty from Russia and Eastern Europe. In this version, ricotta and mascarpone spiked with orange replace the traditional farmer's cheese filling. The blintzes can be prepared in advance and heated just before serving. To achieve the best-sized blintzes, use a 10-inch skillet for the pancakes.

For the Filling

Combine the ingredients except for flour until smooth. Add flour if needed to thicken (the filling should not be runny). Refrigerate for at least 1 hour.

For the Pancakes

Place milk, eggs, flour, and salt in a blender. Blend on low speed until smooth, about 1 minute. Refrigerate for at least 30 minutes.

Warm a 10-inch nonstick skillet over medium-high heat. Brush with a thin coat of melted butter. When butter begins to smoke, lift and tilt the pan to one side and pour a thin stream of batter on the higher side, swirling and tilting to just thinly coat the bottom of the pan. Place the pan flat on the heat and cook until the pancake top is set, the edges begin to dry and pull away from the sides of the pan, and the bottom is golden. Loosen the edges gently with a spatula and turn the blintz over onto a paper towel or piece of wax paper, golden side up. Cover with a thin towel. Repeat with remaining batter. Cooked pancakes can be stored in the refrigerator for a day.

For the Blueberry Sauce

Combine the sugar and cornstarch in a medium saucepan. Stir in the blueberries to coat, and then stir in the water. Warm the mixture over medium heat, then increase heat, bring to a boil, and stir constantly until the mixture thickens and the blueberries are soft, about 10 minutes. Off heat, stir in orange juice to taste and add sugar if needed. Serve warm, or refrigerate and reheat when ready to use.

For the Blintzes

Generously butter a large glass baking dish. Move oven rack to top position and preheat the oven to 450 degrees.

Put about 3 tablespoons of filling in the center of a pancake. Fold the bottom up across the filling, then fold in the sides and fold down the top to completely enclose the filling. Place seam-side down in the baking dish. Repeat with remaining pancakes. At this point, blintzes can be refrigerated until ready to use.

In a small bowl, combine the topping ingredients (butter, brown sugar, and cornstarch). Gently press a little of the topping on top of each blintz.

Bake on uppermost rack in oven for 5 to 6 minutes (longer if the blintzes were refrigerated), until the topping begins to melt. Broil 3 to 4 minutes, until the blintzes are puffy and lightly browned on the edges and the topping is bubbly. Remove and let cool slightly.

Serve warm on individual plates topped with blueberry sauce and a dusting of confectioners' sugar.

Yield: 12 to 14 blintzes (Dairy)

---

6 hard-cooked eggs, peeled and halved lengthwise

1 tablespoon grated Parmigiano-Reggiano cheese

1/4 cup mayonnaise or light mayonnaise

1 teaspoon Dijon mustard

1 teaspoon white wine vinegar

Salt and freshly ground black pepper

12 pieces Parmigiano-Reggiano cheese, thinly sliced and about 1-inch square

12 slivers of smoked salmon (about 1 ounce)

1 1/2 tablespoons chopped fresh dill

Stuffed Eggs with Parmesan, Smoked Salmon, and Dill

Here's a Jewish-Italian riff on stuffed eggs. Use good-quality Parmigiano-Reggiano cheese. Light mayonnaise works just fine.

Remove the egg yolks and mash in a bowl. Stir in 1 tablespoon of Parmigiano-Reggiano cheese, and then the mayonnaise, mustard, and vinegar. Taste and season with salt and pepper if needed.

Stuff each egg white with a spoonful of the yolk mixture. Insert one corner of a cheese slice into the yolk mixture. Place a piece of smoked salmon alongside the cheese. Repeat with remaining eggs. Sprinkle with dill and chill covered for about 1 hour before serving.

Yield: 12 stuffed eggs (Dairy)

Chapter 8

Passover

Outside Israel, Passover typically entails two Seders—the services that commemorate the story of the Jews' exodus from Egypt—and totals eight days of observance. The food is most notable for what we leave out—bread, and anything related (in remembrance of the Jews who fled Egypt so quickly that their bread couldn't rise and instead stayed flat and dry—today's matzah).

It always feels like a brainteaser to choose recipes and create menus for the Passover Seders and the remaining days of the holiday. But it's made me creative. I adapted Italian dishes like chicken cacciatora and potato gnocchi. For desserts, I created a chocolate marshmallow pie and a banana tart plus fudgy brownies (the latter two being gluten free as well kosher for Passover).

Remember that most products (including marshmallows and parchment paper) must be certified kosher for Passover. Always check with your own trusted authorities for guidance.

Reflections
THE PASSOVER DIARIES

Recipes
PASSOVER GNOCCHI WITH PEPPER AND TOASTED GARLIC

PEPPER AND TOMATO QUINOA PILAF

CHICKEN CACCIATORA

LEEK AND MUSHROOM FARFEL KUGEL

MATZAH-RELLA PIZZA

MATZAH BREI (FRIED MATZAH) WITH PARMESAN AND BASIL

APPLE-CINNAMON HAROSET

COCONUT CHOCOLATE PASSOVER DREAM PIE

RICH FLOURLESS BROWNIES

MATZAH CRUNCH

BANANA MARSHMALLOW TART

The Passover Diaries

Year 1: Hello, Matzah!

It's my first Passover dinner. Daryl's parents, very soon to be my in-laws, have invited me to their home in southern California for the holiday. David, Daryl's dad, leads the service. He might well be the shortest person in terms of height, but he commands the table of 14 with his outsized knowledge and love of Jewish history and culture.

With gentle determination, he nudges everyone to find meaning in the historical ritual of Passover—even, and perhaps especially, me, whom he calls on for what he knows to be a nontraditional reading about Judaism's very first Jew by choice, Ruth. It's a kind welcoming gesture, although I feel my heart racing at being shoved into the spotlight at my first Seder.

As we prepare to eat—finally—I gaze at the expanse of food. When no one is looking, I crinkle my forehead. I don't think I like matzah, the main food for the eight-day Passover holiday and the dominant ingredient in many Passover holiday foods. Although matzah balls seem quite enjoyable, especially because this particular year they've come out nice and firm, almost like a big ball of pasta. (And I have come to find that a little bath in chicken soup seems to do matzah a lot of good.)

But across the buffet of nearly all brown food, most of the traditional dishes revolve around matzah. One that does not is gefilte fish. I like fish, I think hopefully. But one whiff of the white fish ground up and packed into a beige oval disk that is preserved in a gel and—oh, never mind. What's a pasta lover to do?

Year 2: The Brisket Kid

One year later, on my second Passover, I want to help and learn the inner workings of the complicated holiday dinner—to better alter it to my liking someday—and I report for kitchen duty. My mother-in-law, Gloria, assigns me to cook the main dish beef brisket with a new recipe she found that uses cranberries and mushrooms.

My father-in-law, David, disappears to the garage to retrieve the meat from the second fridge. He rounds the corner back to the kitchen with arms full of perhaps the biggest single cut of meat I have ever seen. I take it and plunk it on the counter, wondering just what I have gotten myself into. Luckily, I'm making the meat the day before the Seder.

An hour or so later, my pan of browned beef, cranberry juice, wine, and rosemary nestles into the large roaster for a long braise. After three hours of cooking, the meat, which should pull apart with a tug from a fork, budged not one bit. Midnight comes, still nothing. Although I have no idea when or even if the brisket will be done, I convince everyone to go to bed because I will surely finish soon. Washing dishes and scrubbing the countertops distract me from the thought that my maiden main dish for the Seder might be a miserable and expensive flop. But, finally, another couple of hours later, a gentle tug frees some meat (and even more to my relief, it tastes good). I transfer the much-diminished slab to a platter, turn around to put it in the fridge, and come face-to-face with Gloria in her nightgown. She looks horrified.

"Marshee! It's 2:30, what are you STILL doing up?"
"I'm just finishing, it took longer than I thought."
She stomps her foot in mock indignation and says, "Get to bed RIGHT NOW!" as she raises her arm and points her finger in the direction of the bedroom.
"But I —"
"Now!"
We giggle. She grabs the platter of cranberry brisket. No match for her, I hurry to bed. I try to forget about my Passover cooking trial, but the entire house smells of beef.

Year 3: My Fair Gnocchi

Flash forward another year, back in David and Gloria's kitchen.

I hope no one comes around the corner right now to see this. I've accidentally created a cloud of matzah cake meal that is settling throughout the kitchen. There are telltale matzah meal handprints on the spice cabinet. And three pots, a cheese-clogged handheld grater, empty tomato sauce cans, a bowl, and a large baking sheet clutter the countertop. The place is a mess.

It's my third Passover, and it's time. Time to introduce something Italian to this holiday festival. Please let it work.

One pot bubbles with a quick tomato sauce, like you would use to coat any pasta. In another pot, steam rises as the salted water begins to boil. I break off little pieces of potato dough and press each dumpling with the back of a fork to give it ridges just like regular gnocchi. And it is almost like regular potato gnocchi except a little matzah cake meal is binding everything together. My dumplings look like gnocchi, and that's a sight to behold during Passover.

A little while later, I bring the large bowl of gnocchi dressed in bright tomato sauce out of the kitchen to the dining room table. My taste-testers take turns spooning out large portions for each of their plates, and after the first bite … they can't believe it's kosher for Passover (that's a high compliment). I sit down with them, enjoying the rare pleasure of eating something chewy and pasta-like during the no-bread holiday. But the best part comes as lunch ends and we rise to clear the table. Not a single gnocchi to be found.

Passover Gnocchi with Pepper and Toasted Garlic

Gnocchi at Passover—how great is that? With some experimenting, I found that matzah cake meal and a little extra pepper produces tender and flavorful (kosher for Passover) potato dumplings that need nothing more than a simple finish with oil, garlic, and red pepper flakes (though you can coat them in any sauce you like). Note that shaping gnocchi is not difficult but takes time. I like making them ahead and freezing them—to serve, it's just a quick boil and then sauté or toss with sauce. Use a potato ricer if you have one to get fluffier potatoes and softer dough.

2 pounds Yukon gold or butter potatoes

³/₄ teaspoon salt

Freshly ground black pepper (¹/₄ teaspoon or more to taste)

1¹/₂ cups matzah cake meal, plus more as needed

¹/₂ cup potato starch

Extra-virgin olive oil

¹/₈ teaspoon crushed red pepper flakes, or to taste

6 large garlic cloves, sliced lengthwise into thirds

1 cup freshly grated Parmesan cheese (optional)

Wash potatoes and cut into large pieces. Boil until just tender, about 20 minutes. Drain. When cool enough to handle, peel and discard skin. Press potatoes through a potato ricer or mash them into a large bowl. Stir in salt and pepper.

Line a baking sheet with parchment paper and set aside.

Gently whisk together the matzah cake meal and potato starch. Fold the dry ingredients into the potatoes, and knead for 1 minute to blend into a smooth but still slightly sticky dough. Add a little cake meal if too moist or sprinkle with water if too dry.

Bring a large pot of salted water to boil while you shape the gnocchi.

Take a small handful of dough and roll into a little rope about ¹/₂-inch thick. Slice the rope into ³/₄-inch pieces. Gently pinch each piece between your finger and the prongs of a fork to give the gnocchi a ribbed texture. Place on the prepared parchment. Repeat until all the dough has been shaped. If not cooking immediately, cover and refrigerate. Gnocchi can also be frozen at this point.

Place a thick (about ¹/₃ inch) layer of olive oil in a wide, shallow bowl (or a couple of pie plates) and set aside. Gently stir half the gnocchi into the boiling water. After about a minute, the dumplings will start rising to the surface. Cook 40 seconds more, taste for doneness (the dumplings should be al dente), and quickly remove with a slotted spoon or small strainer to the bowl with the oil, stirring gently to coat to prevent sticking. Repeat with remaining gnocchi.

After all gnocchi are cooked, heat a layer of extra-virgin olive oil in a large, nonstick skillet over medium-high heat. Stir in red pepper flakes and some of the garlic pieces, and then place as many gnocchi as will fit in one layer in the pan. Cook until both sides are golden brown and crisped, 6 to 10 minutes (remove the garlic sooner if it is getting too brown). Remove to a warmed platter and top with cheese if using. Repeat with remaining gnocchi. Serve immediately.

Yield: 4 to 5 dinner servings (Pareve without cheese; Dairy if topped with cheese)

Extra-virgin olive oil

³/₄ cup finely chopped sweet onion

Kosher salt and freshly ground black pepper

²/₃ cup finely chopped yellow bell pepper

²/₃ cup seeded and chopped tomato (about 1 medium tomato)

2 cups coarsely chopped baby spinach

1 cup quinoa (rinsed if package directions call for it)

2 cups chicken broth

³/₄ cup coarsely chopped walnuts, preferably toasted

Pepper and Tomato Quinoa Pilaf

In recent years, quinoa has become popular for its versatility, high protein content, and nutty flavor among other good reasons. Huge bonus: this "grain," which is really a seed, is considered by most authorities to be kosher for Passover. All that makes it worth exploring, and here's a "pilaf" for starters. My version uses pepper, tomato, spinach, and walnuts. Good and good for you, year round. It's also gluten-free.

Heat a layer of olive oil in a medium saucepan over medium-high heat. Add the onion and sprinkle with salt and pepper. Cook 1 to 2 minutes until just starting to soften. Add the yellow pepper and tomato, sprinkle lightly with salt, and cook, stirring frequently, another 1 to 2 minutes. Add spinach and turn a few times until wilted.

Add a little more oil if mixture seems dry, and stir in the quinoa. Cook for another minute, stirring constantly. Add the broth and bring mixture to a boil. Reduce heat, cover, and simmer for 15 to 20 minutes, until liquid is mostly absorbed. Remove from heat and let stand 5 minutes. Fluff grains with a fork and gently stir in walnuts.

Yield: About 7½ cups, or 5 to 7 side-dish servings (Meat)

Passover Notes: Most authorities consider quinoa kosher for Passover. However, some require that the quinoa be processed at a plant that does not also handle wheat products or that the quinoa be certified kosher for Passover. Check with your rabbi for guidance.

Note: See photo at the top of p. 137.

3 large bell peppers (ideally 1 each of red, orange, and yellow), halved

Extra-virgin olive oil

Canola or other good frying oil

A 4-pound chicken, cut up, or 4 pounds mixed skin-on, bone-in chicken pieces, patted dry

Kosher salt and freshly ground black pepper

1 large red onion, halved and sliced (about 2 cups)

2 large garlic cloves, sliced thin

1 tablespoon matzah cake meal (or all-purpose flour when not Passover)

1/2 cup dry white wine (such as Pinot Grigio)

1 can (28 ounces) diced tomatoes (preferably fire-roasted) with their juices

1/2 cup no-salt added tomato sauce

1/3 cup fresh basil leaves, chopped (optional)

Chicken Cacciatora

Colorful, tender, flavorful "hunter's style" chicken did not originate as a Passover dish. But I find the Italian tomato-braised chicken stew a welcome addition to the holiday table. I like adding roasted peppers for their color and sweetness. For best results, allow yourself time to cook the stew over very low heat (see note). You can also make it ahead and gently reheat before serving.

Preheat the broiler. Arrange the peppers cut side down on a baking pan covered with foil. Brush the peppers lightly with olive oil. Broil until the skins are mostly blackened (8 to 15 minutes). Remove and cover with foil for about 15 minutes. Remove and discard charred skins and slice the peppers into strips.

Heat a layer of canola oil in a large nonstick pan with a lid (preferably a Dutch oven) over medium-high heat. Add a single layer of chicken pieces and season lightly with salt and generously with pepper. Brown both sides. Remove and repeat with remaining chicken. When cool enough to handle, remove and discard the skin (this keeps the stew from being greasy).

Add the onion to the empty pan and sprinkle lightly with salt. Cook, stirring frequently, over medium heat and scraping browned bits from the bottom of the pan until the onion starts to soften (2 to 5 minutes). Add the garlic, and cook, stirring constantly, for 1 minute, until fragrant. Sprinkle the cake meal or flour over the vegetables, and cook, stirring constantly, for 30 to 45 seconds. Stir in the wine, tomatoes, sauce, pepper strips, and chicken and its accumulated juices, submerging the chicken. Cover loosely and simmer over low heat, stirring a couple of times, until chicken is tender and at an internal temperature of 165 degrees (about 40 to 50 minutes, but longer if heat is very low). Remove from heat and stir in the basil. (If making ahead, wait to add the basil until just before serving.)

Yield: 6 to 8 servings (Meat)

Note: To cook over very low heat, a flame tamer or heat diffuser can help moderate the heat on the stovetop. Use an instant-read thermometer to monitor doneness and adjust heat as needed to keep the cooking on track for your timetable.

Extra-virgin olive oil

5 cups matzah farfel

4 large eggs, lightly beaten

3 garlic cloves, pressed or minced

1/8 teaspoon crushed red pepper flakes

3 cups coarsely chopped leek bulbs and light green parts (about 3 large leeks)

1 large sweet onion, finely chopped

Kosher salt and freshly ground black pepper

3 cups sliced mixed mushrooms (such as shiitake, portobello, or button)

1/4 cup dry white wine, like Pinot Grigio

3 3/4 cups chicken broth

Leek and Mushroom Farfel Kugel

Matzah farfel (little bits) comes out divinely pasta- and stuffing-like in this baked dish flavored with leeks, onions, mushrooms, and chicken stock. Plan to let the casserole rest at room temperature for 10 to 20 minutes before serving. Note that the size of matzah farfel varies among brands—and smaller farfel pieces (about the size of the tip of your index finger, such as Streit's brand) work best for this dish.

Preheat the oven to 400 degrees. Coat a 9-by-13-inch glass baking dish with olive oil.

Heat a thin layer of olive oil in large nonstick skillet over medium-high heat. Add the farfel and eggs, and turn with a spatula until the eggs are absorbed, 3 to 5 minutes. Transfer to prepared baking dish.

Wipe out the skillet, return it to the heat, and warm a thin layer of oil. Add garlic and crushed red pepper flakes and cook for 15 to 30 seconds, stirring constantly, until fragrant. Add the leeks and onions, and season lightly with salt and pepper. Cook, stirring occasionally, until softened, 3 to 5 minutes. Remove the vegetables to a plate.

Wipe skillet again, return to the heat, and add oil. Sauté mushrooms, seasoned lightly with salt and pepper, until softened and lightly browned, 2 to 5 minutes. Add the onions and leeks back to the pan, and stir in the wine. Cook, stirring frequently, for 2 minutes, until thick and bubbly. Transfer contents of skillet to dish with farfel. Stir to combine well and then smooth the top. Pour the chicken broth over top, and nudge the mixture gently with a spoon to distribute the liquid evenly.

Bake for 25 to 30 minutes, until lightly browned on top (some liquid will still be bubbling). Remove from the oven and let rest 10 to 20 minutes before serving. Can be cut into loose squares or spooned out.

The kugel can also be refrigerated or frozen. Reheat cold or frozen pieces loosely placed in an uncovered glass baking dish at 350 degrees for 20 to 30 minutes or until hot.

Yield: About 12 side-dish servings (Meat)

Matzah-rella Pizza

5 to 6 large unsalted matzahs

Extra-virgin olive oil

1 jar (14 ounces) pizza sauce

2 cups (approximate) sautéed, steamed, or roasted sliced or chopped vegetables, such as red and green bell peppers, mushrooms, zucchini, red onions, seeded jalapeños, or broccoli

2 cups shredded part-skim mozzarella cheese

3/4 cup freshly grated Parmesan cheese

3/4 cup part-skim ricotta or cottage cheese (optional)

Matzah pizza (a brainstorm of my husband's), as unusual as it sounds, always gets eaten. And it gives us a chance to goof off in the kitchen, dousing the very staid matzah with zesty sauce and choosing the toppings depending on our mood. Toasting the matzah before adding the toppings helps it hold its own against the sauce a little longer.

Preheat the oven to 450 degrees.

Line 2 baking sheets with foil. Cover each pan with matzah pieces. Brush on a light coating of olive oil. Transfer to oven and toast about 4 minutes, until matzah is dry on top but not browning. Remove and reduce heat to 375 degrees.

Spoon a thin layer of sauce over the matzah. Top with mozzarella, then vegetables, then Parmesan, and, finally, small mounds of ricotta every few inches.

Bake for 5 to 10 minutes, until cheese melts. Serve right away (the matzah softens quickly).

Yield: 6 to 8 servings (Dairy)

Passover Notes: Use kosher for Passover prepared sauce or make your own quick marinara (see recipe p. 73).

6 large matzahs, broken into approximately 1- to 1½-inch pieces

4 large eggs

2½ tablespoons milk

½ teaspoon salt, or to taste

¼ to ½ teaspoon freshly ground black pepper, or to taste

2 tablespoons unsalted butter

⅓ cup finely chopped onion (about half a medium-sized onion)

½ cup freshly grated Parmesan cheese

¼ cup chopped fresh basil leaves

Matzah Brei (Fried Matzah) with Parmesan and Basil

Frying matzah with eggs turns it into a sweet or savory breakfast. For me, savory is the way to go, especially with a little Italian accent of Parmesan cheese and fresh basil. The ratio of matzah to eggs is a matter of personal taste; here's what I think creates the right texture and flavor. I don't recommend substituting whole wheat matzah here because it tends to overwhelm the other flavors.

Place the matzah pieces in a colander in the sink. Bring about 4 cups of water to boil. Slowly pour the hot water over the matzah, shaking the colander to drain.

In a large bowl, lightly beat the eggs, milk, salt, and pepper with a fork. Stir in the moistened matzah pieces to coat well.

Melt butter until bubbly in a large nonstick skillet over medium-high heat. Add the onion, and cook, stirring frequently, until just softened, 1 to 2 minutes. Stir in matzah. Cook, turning occasionally with a spatula, until the matzah pieces are lightly browned, 4 to 7 minutes. Reduce heat to low, sprinkle with cheese and basil and cook covered loosely with foil until cheese melts, 1 to 2 minutes more. Serve hot.

Yield: 4 to 5 servings (Dairy)

Apple-Cinnamon Haroset

3 cups shredded Fuji apple (about 3 large apples), drained

1 cup chopped walnuts

1 teaspoon ground cinnamon

1/3 to 1/2 cup Concord grape kosher for Passover sweet wine

Haroset is a fresh and simple apple, nut, and wine salad key to the Seder service, but delicious in its own right (try it as a side dish or ice cream topping). Many families have their own special versions; this is how my father-in-law, David, makes it—and I've seen more than one person sneak a second (or third) helping during the Seder. Leaving the skin on the apples saves some work and adds color to the final dish.

Add the apples and walnuts to a medium bowl. Sprinkle cinnamon over and gently toss. Stir in about 1/3 cup of wine and add more as needed to evenly coat. Cover and refrigerate. Let stand at room temperature for 30 minutes or so before serving.

Yield: About 3½ cups (Pareve)

Crust

1 package (7 ounces) sweetened coconut flakes

½ cup finely chopped pecans or walnuts

1 tablespoon sugar

½ teaspoon ground cinnamon

1 teaspoon vanilla or vanilla flavoring

2 tablespoons unsalted margarine, melted

Filling

1 cup coconut or almond milk

4 cups miniature marshmallows

1 tablespoon unsalted margarine, melted

1 teaspoon vanilla or vanilla flavoring

4 ounces nondairy bittersweet chocolate, broken into pieces

1 cup nondairy whipping cream, chilled (available in kosher markets)

Topping

2 tablespoons toasted coconut, reserved from crust preparation

1 cup miniature marshmallows, toasted (see note)

2 ounces nondairy bittersweet chocolate, melted, for drizzling (optional)

Coconut Chocolate Passover Dream Pie

Here, a creamy chocolate marshmallow filling rests between a toasty coconut crust and a topping of chocolate, toasted marshmallows, and coconut—one of my first Passover originals. If you don't need to go nondairy, you can use butter and regular whipping cream in the recipe.

Preheat the oven to 350 degrees.

Place the coconut flakes on a large rimmed baking sheet. Toast for 5 to 9 minutes, stirring every 2 minutes, and then every minute after they start to brown. When most flakes are golden brown, remove the pan and set aside to cool.

Set aside 2 tablespoons of the toasted coconut for topping the pie. Crush the remaining flakes into smaller pieces (enough to give about 1¾ cups of crumbs). Combine the coconut, nuts, sugar, and cinnamon in a medium-sized bowl. Add the vanilla to the melted margarine, and then stir the margarine mixture into the coconut mixture until incorporated. Press into bottom and sides of an 8- or 9-inch pie dish. Bake at 350 degrees for 8 to 11 minutes, until warmed and lightly browned. Remove to a wire rack to cool.

To make the filling, combine the milk and marshmallows in a heavy, medium-sized saucepan over low heat. Stir frequently until melted and smooth. Transfer marshmallow mixture to a metal bowl. Stir in the melted margarine, vanilla, and chocolate. Allow the mixture to cool and thicken slightly, whisking occasionally to incorporate as the chocolate melts, 5 to 10 minutes.

Beat the whipping cream using an electric mixer until it holds soft peaks. Gently fold the cream into the marshmallow mixture. Pour mixture into pie plate, cover, and refrigerate for at least 6 hours. Up to a couple of hours before serving, top with reserved toasted coconut and toasted marshmallows. Drizzle melted chocolate over top. Refrigerate until ready to serve.

Yield: 1 pie, 8 to 10 slices (Pareve)

Note: To toast the marshmallows for garnish, spread them on a cookie sheet lined with aluminum foil and coated with cooking spray. Toast in a 350-degree oven until golden brown. Remove from oven and let the marshmallows cool in the pan. When cool, they will be crispy and you can break them apart.

Passover Notes: One option for adding crunch and flavor is sprinkling ¾ cup chopped dry-roasted peanuts over the crust before adding the filling—but authorities disagree about using peanuts during Passover, so check before using them.

Rich Flourless Brownies

1/2 pound (2 sticks) butter, plus more for pan

8 ounces good-quality bittersweet chocolate

4 large eggs

1/2 teaspoon salt

1 cup firmly packed dark brown sugar

1 cup granulated sugar

2 teaspoons vanilla extract or flavoring

Dash of ground cinnamon

1 cup finely ground blanched almonds or almond flour (see note)

1/4 cup potato starch

These brownies have all the bases covered. First, they taste chocolate-y rich without a hint of matzah (there's none in them). Second, they are kosher for Passover thanks to substituting almond flour and potato starch for flour. Third, that also makes them gluten free, and they have been a big hit with friends following a gluten-free diet.

Butter a 9-by-13-inch baking dish and line with buttered aluminum foil or parchment paper (when not Passover, use cooking spray if desired). Preheat the oven to 350 degrees.

Melt the butter and chocolate together in a double boiler or the microwave. Cool slightly.

Whisk the eggs in a large bowl. Whisk in salt, sugars, vanilla, and cinnamon.

In a different bowl, whisk together the ground almonds or almond flour and potato starch.

Whisk chocolate mixture into egg mixture, then fold in the almond mixture until just combined. Pour batter into prepared pan, and bake for 35 to 45 minutes or until shiny and beginning to brown at edges.

Cool completely in the pan on a wire rack before cutting, or serve still warm from the pan with ice cream.

Yield: 15 large or 24 small brownies (Dairy)
Note: A 6-ounce bag of slivered blanched almonds grinds into about 1¼ cups.

Matzah Crunch

5 to 6 unsalted regular or whole wheat matzahs

1/2 pound (2 sticks or 1 cup) unsalted butter or margarine

1 cup firmly packed light brown sugar

1 1/2 cups semisweet chocolate chips (or more if you like it chocolate-y)

Toffee and chocolate transform humble matzah into a crunchy confection—very simply, it's the best use of matzah that I know of. One suggestion—make lots! Also, use butter for the best taste and texture. I sometimes use whole wheat matzah and like it just fine, though its stronger flavor and coarseness sometimes is noticeable (the results vary by brand). Adapted from Marcy Goldman's wonderful signature recipe (found in A Treasury of Jewish Holiday Baking*).*

Preheat the oven to 350 degrees.

Line 2 cookie sheets completely with foil, then line bottoms with parchment paper (this will make it easier to lift the crunch out of the pan and clean up the hardened caramel later). Place the matzahs evenly in a single layer over the parchment, using smaller or broken pieces of matzah to fill any gaps.

Place the butter or margarine and the sugar in a medium saucepan over medium heat. Cook, stirring constantly, until boiling. Boil for 3 minutes, stirring constantly. Pour over the matzahs and spread to cover the matzahs completely.

Bake for 12 to 15 minutes, checking every few minutes until nicely browned. If browning too quickly, rotate the pans or lower the heat to 325 degrees.

Remove from the oven and quickly sprinkle the chocolate chips over top. Let stand for about 5 minutes, then spread the melted chocolate across the top. Place the pans in the freezer; chill until set. Remove, break the matzah crunch into pieces, and bring to room temperature before storing in an airtight container.

Yield: 30 to 40 medium-sized pieces (Dairy)
Note: See photo at the top of the next page.

Banana Marshmallow Tart

Crust
1 cup very finely chopped walnuts

1 cup almond flour or very finely chopped blanched almonds

1 teaspoon potato starch

$1/8$ teaspoon salt

1 tablespoon margarine, melted

Filling
$1/2$ cup (1 stick) margarine

1 bag (10 ounces) plus 3 cups miniature or large marshmallows

$1\frac{3}{4}$ cups mashed very ripe banana (about 5 medium bananas)

$1/2$ teaspoon salt

Topping
3 firm ripe bananas, peeled and cut in half lengthwise

2 tablespoons margarine, plus more as needed

$1/8$ teaspoon salt

3 tablespoons light brown sugar

$1/2$ teaspoon vanilla or vanilla flavoring

$1/8$ teaspoon (generous) ground cinnamon

Pinch of ground nutmeg

This is one of my favorite Passover dessert creations—its banana-caramel-marshmallow creaminess looks and tastes impressive in a way that pleases both grownups and kids. I like the combined flavor of walnuts and almonds in the crust, but you can use just one or the other. Added virtues: This can be made as a gluten- and dairy-free dessert option for whenever you need one, and it's best made the night before serving. Note that you'll need one full bag and part of a second bag of marshmallows. Also note that you need both firm and very ripe bananas, about 8 total.

For the Crust
Preheat the oven to 350 degrees. Spread the walnuts and almonds on a baking sheet and toast for about 8 minutes, stirring every few minutes, until fragrant. Let cool slightly. Transfer to a bowl and stir in potato starch and salt. Blend in melted margarine. Firmly press this mixture on the bottom of a 10-inch round tart dish or similar. Bake crust for about 8 minutes. Remove to a wire rack to cool.

For the Filling
Melt the $1/2$ cup of margarine over medium heat in a large saucepan or soup pot. Add the marshmallows, and stir frequently until melted. Remove from heat. Stir in mashed banana and salt, and pour over the crust. Let cool slightly, then cover and freeze just until set, about 30 minutes.

For the Topping
Cut each banana length into 4 or 5 pieces. Melt 2 tablespoons of margarine in a large nonstick skillet, and sprinkle with $1/8$ teaspoon salt, swirling to combine. Add the banana pieces, cut side down, and cook over medium-low heat, 3 to 5 minutes, until just becoming tender (add more margarine if mixture gets too dry). Turn and cook another few minutes, until bananas are tender but not mushy. Remove from heat and sprinkle with brown sugar, vanilla, cinnamon, and nutmeg. Turn gently with a spatula to coat bananas.

Let cool slightly, then arrange bananas on top of the marshmallow filling, then drizzle with the syrup from the pan. Cover and refrigerate until ready to serve.

Yield: About 10 servings (Pareve)

Chapter 9

Desserts

I'm not sure whether I got my sweet tooth from my dad's Sicilian ancestry or my maternal heritage of excellent bakers. Either way, I'm a devotee of desserts and sweets, both making and eating them. In college, when others threw keg parties, my roommates and I threw a homemade apple pie party. And my love of apples continues, with two apple desserts here (in addition to the apple challah bread pudding in the eggs and cheese chapter).

The apple crostata has become my favorite Rosh Hashanah finale. But there's much more here than apples. My Italian cannoli recipe includes chocolate and strawberry fillings that create pretty and palate-pleasing variety. My hamantashen (Jewish pastries) break the mold—with chocolate, cream cheese, and Italian hazelnut paste—in a good way (so good that two of my recipe testers now make them for company).

To *la dolce vita!*

Bittersweet

I love cooking for people, but there are those whom I can no longer cook for, except in my very vivid imagination. If I could make one grand feast for all the people I miss, I picture it going like this:

The place, a farmhouse, welcomes. It has floors worn down by thousands of footsteps. Its ceilings, high and beamed, give the rooms air and light. Brown, red, and gold color the house and the furnishings. Goblets of blue glass, soft and clear, adorn the table. Flowers that normally don't exist in the same season sit randomly in terra cotta vases. There are late summer goldenrod, drooping with feathery flaxen stems. Honeysuckle scents the air. Purple irises stand at attention. Taking the glory are white roses, puffy with sweetness and life.

The yard overlooks a valley, lush from sunshine and rain, and shaped by a stream. Mountains rise in the distance beyond, just far away enough to cast a smoky haze in the early evening's sky. Like a monument in the middle of the yard, a weeping willow tree drapes graceful branches in a wide sweep. They almost hide a swing, a wide board strung to the tree with two thick braids of rope.

A large patio of irregularly shaped flagstones is the focal point. Its large table of seasoned wood is inlaid with cream-colored porcelain that shows a flowing vine of blue and pink. The chairs around the table have soft seats with tall backs, comfortable for lingering over food, wine, and conversation.

My father, Berney, would get the place of honor at the head of the table. I'd decorate his place setting with a miniature fishing rod to remind him of the serenity that he always enjoyed standing waterside, casting for trout and bass. I'd also include a few pieces of his favorite candy, bittersweet dark chocolate. I'd want to show him how I adapted his tomato sauce and chili and see whether he approved. I would cook by myself, for him. For so long, he did all the providing. When he became terribly sick, I was mostly away at college. I owe him many dinners. But first, I'd take a couple of frosty beers over to the swing under the willow tree, and we'd swing awhile and catch up. I'd ask questions about his childhood, what was most important, and what event in his life gave him the very best belly laugh he ever had.

A place at the table would be set for my dear friend and bridesmaid Michele, who died way too soon. At Michele's place, I would lay a stargazer lily, one of her favorite flowers. I would want to prepare a meal for her, but part of the fun would be making it with her because she was Italian and loved to cook. Sometimes I think I'm a perfectionist, but she beat me easily in this category. Maybe we could laugh at our fussiness as we worked, and we could let it go. We'd both be the better for it.

What to make? Something Italian, of course. Ziti? Stuffed shells? My father's sauce or her grandmother's sauce? Stuffed peppers? Yes, all of it. She loved my recipe for chili, so I would make that by myself, just for her.

I'd expect my canine companions to show up, too, and I'd be ready. For my grandmother's German Shepherd, I'd have spaghetti doused with Dad's sauce because that was the only way she liked it. I'd want to ask what it was about running as fast as she could and jumping into the swimming hole in the creek that made it worth doing every time she had the chance, without regard to punishment.

Randy, our lovable golden retriever/Labrador mix, would first and foremost accompany me on a nice long walk, through the neighborhoods and trails, across streams balancing on the bodies of fallen trees, just like we used to do. This time I wouldn't let him fall in the water and get soaked. He'd want to sit up and "beg" for his food because he could hold that pose most elegantly, and I'd have ready little bites of steak, pita, and maybe some cheese for him to straighten up for.

Our black-and-white pit bull/Labrador mix Costello, a truly handsome guy, would receive a fine sirloin steak, all for him, like the one he ate off the counter when I wasn't looking, depriving us of meat for our kebobs. I'd give him a sofa pillow, like the one he always used to grab when he wanted our attention, and I'd chase him around as much as he wanted.

For our Tigra, a brindle and muscular mutt with a huge heart, I would make bread. Specifically, challah bread because when we broke bread on Friday night, she rushed for her place right between us and would quiver in anticipation of her piece. I would throw toys for her so she could spin around in tight circles like she did when she was excited—and like she did when we first met her at the homeless animals shelter and decided to adopt her.

Grandma, Aunt Anne, and Uncle Jimmie would sit together. I'd serve them spaghetti and meatballs (I'd need plenty of this dish because it's a favorite) because that's what they always loved most to eat. I'd like to finally get to the bottom of the question of how Grandma became such a pistol. Maybe I'd tease them all for letting it happen, and together we could laugh about it.

For my Gram, my mom's mother, the first thing we'd do together is walk into the grassy fields and pick more goldenrod to bring into the house. It was her tradition and her mother's tradition to bring the wildflower that lights the fields in September inside for good luck every year. I continued to do this after she passed, but it never felt quite the same without her. I would also have her teach me to tell stories; she was a pro, even in her late years, when she began to tell the same stories over again. She'd start to tell a story and pause, a flicker of doubt crossing her mind. "Have I told you this one?" she'd ask. I'd wrinkle my forehead a moment as if to think and then lie a little: "I don't think so." It was always fun to hear her retell the stories.

Making food for her would be tough. I wonder whether it would be okay if I made her favorite, a baked pork chop, something that is not kosher. Doing it for Gram seemed worthy of an exception. I'd serve it with latkes, which I'm sure she would love, because she and I always agreed that potatoes tasted the best when they were fried.

Daryl's Aunt Sylvia's place would be set in pink roses and a pink napkin because pink captured her gentleness that had just a touch of fire. I'd say to her, "Hi, how are ya, doll?" just like she would so often greet those she loved. The desserts would be dedicated to Aunt Sylvia's sweetness. She loved my rugelach, and I'd have a cheesecake to remind her of her daughter Nita, whose cheesecakes she adored.

Even though I didn't know Daryl's grandfather Jacob, I would hope that he would stop by. I'd have plenty to talk with him about, especially his experiences saving his family during World War II. From all accounts, he was a very serious man, and he had every right to be, given what his life and faith had demanded of him. So I'd like to know what in his life made him the happiest. What made him smile? Perhaps I'd sit him between Gram, who could tell him a few stories and laugh along with him, and Aunt Sylvia, who liked to sneak in little witticisms that you didn't see coming and that you couldn't help but giggle at. Because whenever I made chicken soup, Daryl would say the house smelled like Grandpa Jacob's house, I'd make Jacob matzah ball chicken soup and hope it lived up to his version.

I'd look forward to seeing each face gathered around the table with the porcelain inlay, each hand grasping a blue goblet that sparkled in the late afternoon sunlight. I'd look at the bounty of food that I could share with them, food that had meaning for us. I'd hope that they would see, through the special recipes and through the shared times at this table and all those before, that their stories, their legacies, would flourish and grow. That they would live on.

And then we'd eat.

Bittersweet Chocolate Torta

Cooking spray

8 ounces bittersweet chocolate

8 ounces semisweet chocolate

¼ pound (1 stick) unsalted butter

3 teaspoons vanilla extract

Dash of cinnamon

Dash of salt

6 large eggs, cold

1 cup cold whipped cream (soft peaks) (about ¾ cup heavy whipping cream will whip to a little more than 1 cup)

Unsweetened cocoa powder for dusting

Berries, mint leaves, whipped cream, edible flowers, or mascarpone for garnish (optional)

Love chocolate? This is for you. Smooth, thick texture and rich flavor land this confection somewhere between fudge and cheesecake. Flourless chocolate desserts live in Jewish and Italian and many other recipe collections, and are especially valuable to Jewish cooks at Passover (just be sure to use kosher for Passover versions of the ingredients). The keys here are using good-quality chocolate, folding the whipped eggs and cream into the chocolate very gently, and baking the cake in a water bath. With the water bath, it's especially important to leak-proof your springform pan with several layers of heavy-duty aluminum foil.

Preheat the oven to 325 degrees. Line the bottom of a 9-inch springform pan with parchment paper and coat inside of the pan with cooking spray. Wrap three layers of heavy-duty aluminum foil around the outside of the pan. Transfer to a larger roasting pan. On the stovetop, bring approximately 4 quarts of water to a boil. Chill the bowl you are going to use for beating the eggs.

Break the chocolate and cut the butter into small pieces. Melt them together, either in the microwave (50 percent power until just melted, stirring every 30 seconds or so) or in a double boiler, until just smooth. Stir in vanilla, cinnamon, and salt. Transfer to a large bowl and let cool slightly.

Place the eggs in the chilled bowl and beat them with an electric mixer at high speed for 5 minutes (the eggs should be foamy and lightened in color). Gently fold (so as not to deflate) the egg mixture into the melted chocolate in 3 additions, blending each time until nearly incorporated. Gently fold in the whipped cream.

Spread batter in the prepared springform pan and smooth the surface. Place the roasting pan in the oven and add the hot water to the roasting pan so that the water comes one-third of the way up the outside of the springform pan.

Bake 45 to 50 minutes, until the top is shiny and dry and the center of the cake reaches 160 degrees on an instant-read thermometer.

Remove the springform pan from the water bath and place pan on a wire rack to cool, removing the foil when cool enough to handle. Cover and refrigerate overnight. To serve, remove pan sides, invert the cake onto a plate, remove pan bottom and parchment paper, and then invert cake back onto a serving plate. Let stand for 30 minutes at room temperature before serving. Dust with cocoa powder and garnish as desired.

Yield: 16 servings (Dairy)

Note: *If you like coffee flavor and have espresso powder, you can add 1 teaspoon espresso powder to the melted chocolate along with the vanilla, cinnamon, and salt.*

Cooking spray

8 tablespoons (1 stick) unsalted butter, softened

6 ounces (about ¾ cup) block-style, fat-free cream cheese, softened

1½ cups sugar

1½ teaspoons vanilla extract

2 large eggs

1½ cups all-purpose flour

1½ teaspoons baking powder

¼ teaspoon salt

¼ cup firmly packed light brown sugar

2 teaspoons ground cinnamon

3 cups chopped peeled Fuji apple (about 3 apples)

Light Apple Cinnamon Cake

No Jewish recipe collection would be complete without an apple cake. I prize this lighter version for its dense, moist crumb and almost creamy (thanks to fat-free cream cheese) apple-cinnamon-vanilla flavor. It can hold its own as a dessert as well as a brunch dish or a snack. Adapted from Cooking Light, *October 1997.*

Preheat the oven to 350 degrees. Coat an 8½-inch springform pan with cooking spray.

Beat butter, cream cheese, sugar, and vanilla with an electric mixer on medium speed until well blended (about 3 minutes). Add eggs and beat well to incorporate. Add flour, baking powder, and salt to the top of creamed mixture and stir this dry ingredient layer once or twice to lightly combine it before beating it in on low speed until just blended.

In a small bowl, combine the brown sugar and cinnamon. Toss 2 tablespoons of the cinnamon mixture with the apples, and then stir the cinnamon apples into the batter. Pour the batter into the prepared pan, smooth the top, and sprinkle evenly with remaining cinnamon mixture.

Bake at 350 degrees for about 1 hour (start checking at 50 minutes), until a toothpick inserted in the center comes out with just a few crumbs. Cool the cake completely on a wire rack before removing from pan. A serrated knife is helpful for slicing.

Yield: About 12 servings (Dairy)

Zuppa Inglese
1 recipe white chocolate custard cream (below)

1/2 cup strawberry preserves

1/2 cup rum (see note)

1 cinnamon stick

2 pounds (about 5 cups) fresh strawberries

1 plain pound cake (at least 16 ounces), sliced into 1/4-inch pieces

1 cup heavy cream

1/2 tablespoon sugar

White Chocolate Custard Cream
6 cups whole milk

2/3 cup cornstarch

2/3 cup sugar

4 egg yolks

4 teaspoons vanilla extract

4 ounces good-quality white chocolate, broken into small pieces

White Chocolate and Strawberry Zuppa Inglese (Italian Trifle)

This is really an English trifle, Italian style. Although the Italian version often uses candied fruit or nuts, I opted for fresh strawberries, and for the custard layer, a white chocolate-infused cream. Cake soaked in rum adds a little textural contrast and spice to the cool, creamy dessert that will serve a crowd. You will need a 2½-quart (or larger) glass bowl.

For the Custard Cream
Warm 5 1/2 cups of the milk in a medium saucepan over medium heat (do not boil). Meanwhile, in a small mixing bowl, mix the cornstarch and sugar. Add the egg yolks and use the back of a spoon to work them into the cornstarch mixture until crumbly. Stirring constantly, gradually add the remaining 1/2 cup milk to the yolk mixture. Stir in the vanilla.

Once the milk in the saucepan is very warm to the touch, gradually stir in the cornstarch mixture. Cook over medium-high heat, stirring constantly, until mixture thickens and a spoonful placed on top holds its shape.

Remove from heat and stir in the white chocolate until it melts. Place a sheet of plastic wrap directly on the surface to prevent a skin from forming. Refrigerate until no longer hot (about 1 1/2 hours).

For the Trifle
Warm the preserves, rum, and cinnamon stick in a small saucepan over low heat. Stir occasionally until the preserves dissolve completely. Remove from heat and let cool slightly (remove and discard cinnamon stick just before using). Meanwhile, wash, hull, and halve the strawberries, reserving a small handful for garnish.

Line the bottom of a 2 1/2-quart or larger deep glass bowl with a layer of cake slices. Brush on a generous layer of the strawberry-rum syrup. Top with 1/3 of the strawberries, leaving some berries visible at sides of bowl. Then add 1/3 of the custard cream. Repeat the steps 2 more times, and top with a layer of cake slices thoroughly moistened with the syrup. Cover tightly with plastic wrap and refrigerate about 24 hours.

Before serving, whip the cream to soft peaks using an electric mixer, adding the 1/2 tablespoon of sugar about halfway through. Uncover the trifle, and top with whipped cream. Decorate with reserved strawberries.

Yield: About 12 servings (Dairy)
Note: If not observing Kosher rules, you can use spiced dark rum for a little more flavor.

Shell

2¼ cups all-purpose flour

¼ cup sugar

½ teaspoon kosher salt

½ pound (2 sticks) cold unsalted butter, cut into small pieces

¼ cup cold water

Filling

7 cups (about 3 pounds) peeled, cored, and thinly sliced apples (such as a mixture of Ginger Gold, Honeycrisp, and Pink Lady)

1 tablespoon fresh lemon juice

½ teaspoon grated lemon zest

Topping

½ cup all-purpose flour

½ cup sugar

½ teaspoon kosher salt

½ teaspoon ground cinnamon

¼ teaspoon ground allspice

¼ teaspoon ground nutmeg

8 tablespoons (1 stick) unsalted butter, cut into small pieces

Apple Crostata

When apples start filling the market shelves in the fall, I start thinking apple desserts—and this Italian-style open-faced tart is always first (I often make it for Rosh Hashanah). The flaky and buttery crust simply wraps up around the fruit scented with lemon, giving all the pleasures of pie in an easier, more rustic package. Combining different types of apples boosts the flavor, but avoid using firm varieties and slice your apples very thinly so they cook through. Adapted from a recipe by Ina Garten in Barefoot Contessa Parties!

Make the pastry shell by combining the flour, sugar, and salt in a large bowl. Using fingers or a pastry blender, work in the butter until it is in pea-sized pieces and well coated with flour. Add the cold water and stir a few times, then gently form dough into a ball. Divide in half and flatten each half into a disk. Wrap each in plastic wrap and refrigerate for 1 hour (or longer) or freeze about 20 minutes.

Toss the sliced apples with the lemon juice and zest.

Make the topping by combining the ingredients in a small food processor and pulsing until crumbly.

Line a baking sheet with parchment paper. Tear off two additional sheets of parchment paper and place them near the work area.

Remove 1 dough disk from the refrigerator (if using the freezer, transfer the remaining disk to the refrigerator). On a lightly floured surface, roll the dough into an approximate 11-inch circle. Transfer to a piece of parchment paper and trim the paper to leave a 1-inch border all around.

Transfer the trimmed parchment and shell immediately to the prepared baking sheet. Place half the apples in the middle of the shell, leaving a 2-inch border. On the apples place half the topping mixture. Gently fold dough edges around apple mound (about three-quarters up the side of mound) pleating where needed.

Repeat with the second disk. Refrigerate the formed pastries, loosely covered with a sheet of wax paper, for about 1 hour. (They can also be frozen at this point.)

Preheat the oven to 450 degrees (see note). Bake until the crust is golden brown, 20 to 30 minutes (longer if frozen).

Remove and let the tarts rest on the pan for about 5 minutes. Carefully transfer the tarts on their parchment circles to a wire rack to cool. Serve warm or at room temperature. Leftovers can be stored in the refrigerator and reheated in a 350-degree oven.

Yield: Two apple tarts, about 6 servings each (Dairy)

Note: Some liquid might seep from the tarts as they bake; if using a rimless baking sheet, line the lower rack of the oven with foil to catch any drips.

Crust

Crust

¹/₄ cup butterscotch chips

1¹/₄ cups crushed graham crackers (about 7¹/₂ whole graham crackers, such as Honey Maid)

1¹/₂ tablespoons all-purpose flour

1¹/₂ tablespoons light brown sugar

1 teaspoon vanilla extract

3 tablespoons unsalted butter, melted

Filling and Topping

20 caramels, quartered (about 1 cup), and spread apart on wax paper to prevent sticking

1 teaspoon plus 1 tablespoon cornstarch

2 packages (8 ounces each) cream cheese, softened

1 cup (scant) sugar

3 large eggs

2¹/₂ teaspoons vanilla extract

¹/₂ tablespoon fresh lemon juice

¹/₂ teaspoon (scant) salt

3 cups (scant) sour cream

¹/₃ cup chopped chocolate English toffee candy bars (such as Heath, about 7 miniature bars) (see note)

Caramel Cheesecake

Thanks to its start in New York Jewish delis, cheesecake is often considered a Jewish dessert, though there are Italian ricotta cheese "cakes," from which the idea likely originated. If I could only choose one, it'd have to be cheesecake, the creamier the better—and especially this one. Butterscotch, caramel, toffee, and ultra creamy cheese create a knockout cake that charms even non-cheesecake people. This recipe uses an 8½-inch springform pan. Baking the cake in a water bath ensures extra creamy results.

Preheat the oven to 350 degrees. Coat the sides and bottom of an 8½-inch springform pan with cooking spray. Line the bottom with parchment paper and spray the paper. To protect the cake in the water bath, tightly wrap a triple layer of heavy-duty aluminum foil around the outside of the pan. Place the springform pan so that it rests flat in a larger roasting pan. On the stovetop, bring approximately 4 quarts of water to a boil.

For the Crust
Chop the butterscotch chips or pulse them in a small food processor. Combine the chips with the graham cracker crumbs, flour, and sugar. Add the vanilla to the melted butter and then add the butter mixture to the dry ingredients, stirring until evenly moistened and crumbly. Press the crumbs into the bottom of the prepared springform pan.

For the Cheesecake
Sprinkle the caramels with 1 teaspoon of cornstarch and toss to coat well.

In a large bowl, beat the cream cheese and sugar with an electric mixer until smooth, 1 to 2 minutes. Blend in 1 tablespoon of cornstarch. Add the eggs, one at a time, beating at medium speed after each addition until well incorporated, then add the vanilla, lemon juice, and salt. Fold in the sour cream until just blended. Fold in the caramels, leaving any loose cornstarch behind. Pour the mixture into the prepared springform pan sitting in the roasting pan.

Transfer roasting pan to the oven. Add the hot water to the larger pan until the water reaches ¹/₃ of the way up the outside of the springform pan. Bake until the cake's outer edges appear set but the middle few inches are still slightly wobbly, 50 to 70 minutes (and an instant-read thermometer inserted halfway into the cake about an inch from the outside edge reads 165 degrees).

Turn off the oven and let the cake cool in the closed oven for 1 hour. Remove to a wire rack and cool to room temperature before refrigerating, covered, until ready to serve.

To serve, remove the sides of the springform pan and invert the cake onto a plate. Remove the pan bottom and the parchment paper, then reinvert the cake onto the serving plate. Sprinkle with chopped toffee bars.

Yield: One 8½-inch cheesecake, about 8 to 10 servings (Dairy)

Note: To quickly chop the toffee bars (and relieve some stress while you're at it), put unwrapped candies in a resealable plastic bag and bash them with a meat mallet or heavy frying pan. The pieces will be unevenly sized, but I like them that way for the top of the cake.

Cannoli Shells

2 cups all-purpose flour

3 tablespoons sugar

½ teaspoon unsweetened cocoa powder

½ teaspoon salt

¼ cup vegetable shortening

1 egg yolk (white reserved)

1 tablespoon white wine vinegar

2 tablespoons sweet liqueur or wine

1 teaspoon vanilla extract

2 to 4 tablespoons cold water

2 quarts of canola oil for frying

Ever had still-warm cannoli (Sicilian fried pastries) filled with plain, chocolate, or strawberry ricotta cheese fillings? Just wait 'til you do. You'll need cannoli tubes (available at kitchen specialty stores) and a round cookie cutter or drinking glass with a diameter about 1 inch shorter than the length of the tubes.

Combine the flour, sugar, cocoa powder, and salt in a large bowl and work in the vegetable shortening with two knives or a pastry blender to achieve a crumbled texture. In a separate bowl, mix the egg yolk, vinegar, liqueur or wine, and vanilla and then stir into the flour mixture. Add cold water 1 tablespoon at a time until dough is smooth and stiff. Knead gently for 1 to 2 minutes. Divide dough in half, flatten both halves into disks, cover with plastic wrap, and let rest at room temperature for about 45 minutes. (Or, wrap each disk tightly in plastic wrap and refrigerate overnight; bring to room temperature before continuing.)

Lightly beat the reserved egg white with a fork and set aside. Heat oil to 350 degrees in a deep-sided frying pan (preferably a Dutch oven).

While oil heats, transfer 1 disk to a lightly floured surface and roll into an 8- to 10-inch circle. Using a cookie cutter or glass, cut circles from the rolled dough. Repeat with the other disk.

Transfer the circles, one at a time, to a clean surface. With the rolling pin, lightly roll over the circle from top to bottom to thin and spread the circle to an oval (a little less than 5 inches long across its longest section). When rolled out, the dough disk should be able to cover most of the length of the tube without hanging over the ends.

Place a cannoli tube crosswise on the circle so that the tube ends extend just past the shorter sides of the oval. Wrap one long edge of the dough tightly around the tube. Brush the outer lip with the beaten egg white. Wrap the other edge of the dough over top. Firmly press the two edges together to seal. Repeat until all the tubes are wrapped.

Fry the cannoli a few at a time until deep golden brown, about 2 minutes. Remove with tongs or a slotted spoon to a paper-towel-lined plate to drain. Remove the tubes immediately by gently gripping the shell with paper towels and pulling the tube with tongs. Once the tubes are cool enough to handle, wipe off excess oil and use them to shape remaining dough circles.

Cooled shells can be stored for a day wrapped in wax paper in an airtight container.

Yield: 10 to 14 medium-sized cannoli shells (Pareve)

Three Fillings for Cannoli

Choose from plain cheese, strawberry, or chocolate, or if you are making a big tray, it's fun to have all three. The strawberry and chocolate build off the cheese version. Use homemade or store-bought cannoli shells.

For Cheese Filling
1/2 cup heavy whipping cream

3 cups whole-milk, fresh ricotta cheese (drained if runny)

7 1/2 tablespoons confectioners' sugar, plus extra for dusting finished cannoli

3 teaspoons vanilla extract

3/8 teaspoon ground cinnamon

6 ounces bittersweet dark chocolate, finely chopped, or miniature semisweet chocolate chips (about 1 cup) (reserve a teaspoon or so of shavings or chips for garnish if desired)

10 to 14 cannoli shells

For Strawberry Filling
Cheese filling ingredients (except for the 6 ounces bittersweet chocolate)

1/4 cup strawberry preserves

2 cups hulled and chopped strawberries

For Chocolate Filling
Cheese filling ingredients

1/4 cup heavy whipping cream

4 ounces semisweet chocolate, broken into pieces

3 tablespoons cocoa powder (for dusting)

For the Cheese Filling
Beat the whipping cream with an electric mixer on high speed until it holds stiff peaks (about 2 minutes). Set aside. In a separate bowl, beat the ricotta on high speed for 1 minute. Add the whipped cream, 7 1/2 tablespoons of confectioners' sugar, vanilla, and cinnamon to the ricotta, and beat on medium-high speed 1 to 2 minutes, until very smooth. Stir in the chopped chocolate.

Use a small spoon to fill the cooled shells with the ricotta filling. Dust the shells with confectioners' sugar and reserved chocolate shavings or chips if desired. Serve immediately (or hold in refrigerator for not more than 1 hour before serving).

For the Strawberry Filling
Prepare the cheese filling recipe, but omit the chopped chocolate, and instead stir in the strawberry preserves until well combined. Fold in the strawberries. Dust filled shells with confectioners' sugar.

For the Chocolate Filling
Combine the heavy whipping cream and semisweet chocolate in a small saucepan over low heat. Stir frequently until chocolate is melted and mixture is well combined. Remove from heat and let cool slightly. Prepare the cheese filling recipe, but before adding the chopped chocolate pieces, fold the melted chocolate-cream mixture into the ricotta filling until well combined. Then fold in the chopped chocolate. Dust filled shells with cocoa powder and sprinkle with chocolate shavings.

Yield: About 5 cups of filling per flavor, each version enough to fill 12 to 14 medium-sized cannoli shells (Dairy)

Almond Mandelbrot-Biscotti with White Chocolate

1 package (7 ounces) marzipan, grated using the large holes on a box grater

1 cup sugar

8 tablespoons (1 stick) unsalted butter, softened

1 cup almond flour or meal or ground blanched almonds

4 large eggs, lightly beaten

2 teaspoons vanilla extract

2 teaspoons almond extract

3 cups all-purpose flour

1 teaspoon baking powder

$1/2$ teaspoon baking soda

$1/2$ teaspoon salt

$1/4$ teaspoon ground cinnamon

1 cup whole almonds, preferably blanched, but with skins is okay

20 ounces good-quality white chocolate, chopped

Italian biscotti and Jewish mandelbrot or almond bread (the latter likely inspired by the biscotti Jews tasted in Italy or received from Romans traveling through Eastern Europe) are both Old World, twice-baked cookies often featuring almonds—but the confluence is just one small reason I love this particular recipe. It enlivens the classic with a crisp but still tender texture and multilayered almond flavor thanks to marzipan (sweetened almond paste). I like adding a white chocolate coating for complementary sweet vanilla notes and contrasting creamy texture—and, oh yes, a very pretty presentation. Adapted from a recipe by Marcy Goldman in A Treasury of Jewish Holiday Baking.

Preheat the oven to 350 degrees. Line 1 large or 2 smaller baking sheets with parchment paper.

Cream the marzipan and sugar in a large bowl (will be lumpy). Add the butter and continue creaming until well combined. Mix in the almond flour or ground almonds, eggs, vanilla, and almond extract until mostly smooth.

Sprinkle the flour, baking powder, baking soda, salt, and cinnamon over the batter and lightly stir the dry ingredients' layer with a whisk before folding it into the batter. Fold in the whole almonds.

Spoon the batter into 2 equal-sized mounds on the parchment-covered baking sheet(s). Using wet hands (to make it easier to work with the sticky dough), shape the dough into two loaves, each 2 to 3 inches wide and 1 inch high. Leave a few inches between the two loaves if using 1 baking sheet because the dough will spread quite a bit during baking.

Bake for 30 to 40 minutes until the loaves are golden brown all over. Remove and slide the parchment and loaves onto a wire rack to cool for 10 minutes. Meanwhile, turn oven to 325 degrees.

One at a time, transfer each loaf to a cutting board and use a long serrated knife to cut on the diagonal $1/2$- to $3/4$-inch slices. Return the cookies, cut side down, to the baking sheet. Bake for another 18 to 22 minutes, turning halfway, until lightly toasted. Remove and cool completely on wire racks.

Set out a large piece of wax paper or parchment paper. Microwave the white chocolate in a bowl in 15-second increments, stirring after each, until the white chocolate is smooth and reads between 86 and 88 degrees on an instant-read thermometer. Quickly dip one end of each cookie (about a third of the cookie) in the chocolate and then place on the wax paper or parchment paper until chocolate is set. Store in an airtight container.

Yield: About 28 to 36 cookies (Dairy)

Note: If you can't find marzipan, you can use almond paste, but add an extra 1 tablespoon sugar and ½ teaspoon almond extract. The resulting biscotti will be a little more crumbly and less nuanced than those with marzipan, but still good.

4 cups crushed chocolate biscotti (14 to 15 ounces packaged biscotti)

¼ teaspoon ground cinnamon

1 teaspoon plus 2 teaspoons vanilla extract

⅓ cup cooled espresso (about 3 shots from the coffee shop) or strong black coffee, divided

6 tablespoons unsalted butter, melted

16 ounces mascarpone

½ cup sour cream

1 cup confectioners' sugar

1½ cups heavy whipping cream

1 tablespoon unsweetened Dutch-process cocoa powder

2 ounces bittersweet chocolate, grated

Semifreddo Tiramisu Squares

My chocolate-mascarpone-espresso creation crosses between a no-bake cheesecake and a tiramisu. Besides the lovely flavors, it offers a pleasing texture of a crumbly biscotti crust topped with a creamy filling. I think these bars are best semi-frozen (semifreddo) or just as they are softening.

Preheat the oven to 350 degrees. Line a 10-by-13-inch glass baking dish with aluminum foil and allow extra to hang over both short edges to ease removing the bars.

Combine the biscotti crumbs and cinnamon. Add 1 teaspoon of the vanilla and 1 teaspoon of the espresso to the melted butter. Stir the butter mixture into the biscotti mixture until crumbs are well coated. Press into the bottom of the prepared baking dish.

Bake for 10 to 15 minutes, until the crust is lightly browned and dry to the touch. Remove to a wire rack.

To make the filling, place the mascarpone in a large bowl and beat lightly with a wooden spoon until smooth. Stir in 2 teaspoons vanilla, 2 teaspoons of espresso, and the ½ cup sour cream. Gradually beat in the confectioners' sugar. In a separate bowl, beat the whipping cream with an electric mixer on high speed until it holds soft peaks. Fold the cream into the mascarpone mixture until just combined.

Lightly brush the remaining espresso over the cooled crust. Cover with the mascarpone filling and smooth the top. Dust with cocoa powder and sprinkle with grated chocolate.

Refrigerate uncovered for 1 to 2 hours, until thoroughly chilled, then cut into rectangles, cover, and freeze overnight. After it sets, can be wrapped tightly and stored in freezer for up to a week. Serve just slightly thawed.

Yield: About 24 bars (Dairy)

Dough

¹/₂ cup (4 ounces) cream cheese, softened

8 tablespoons (1 stick) unsalted butter, softened

1 teaspoon vanilla

¹/₂ cup sugar

1¹/₂ cups all-purpose flour, plus additional as needed

1 teaspoon baking powder

3 tablespoons unsweetened Dutch-process cocoa powder

¹/₈ teaspoon salt

Dash of cinnamon

Pastries

¹/₂ cup (4 ounces) cream cheese, softened

¹/₂ teaspoon vanilla

¹/₂ cup confectioners' sugar

Dash of cinnamon

¹/₂ cup (generous) Nutella (hazelnut chocolate spread)

1 egg white and a pinch of salt, lightly beaten together with a fork

Coarse sugar, like turbinado, or regular sugar for topping

Chocolate Cream-Cheese Hazelnut Hamantashen

Hamantashen are Jewish triangle-shaped pastries, usually a blond dough filled with fruit or poppy-seed filling. Good, yes, but ... a chocolate–cream cheese dough and an Italian hazelnut chocolate spread (Nutella) filling make them flaky, creamy, and a little decadent—my kind of pastry. Although hamantashen are tied to the early spring holiday of Purim, we enjoy my chocolate rendition year round.

To make the dough, cream the cheese and butter until smooth. Stir in vanilla and ¹/₂ cup of sugar. Add flour, baking powder, cocoa powder, salt, and cinnamon, and blend to form a soft dough. If too sticky to handle, add a little more flour. Gather the dough into a loose ball and transfer to a large piece of plastic wrap. Flatten dough to a large disk, wrap in the plastic, and refrigerate for approximately 1 hour (this will make rolling easier).

Preheat the oven to 350 degrees. Line a baking sheet with parchment paper.

In a small bowl, combine the cream cheese, vanilla, confectioners' sugar, and cinnamon until smooth.

To make the pastries, unwrap the dough and place it on a large piece of parchment paper. With a rolling pin lightly dusted with flour, roll the dough to about ¹/₄ inch thick or a little less. Use a 3-inch drinking glass or cookie cutter to cut rounds, then gently lift and replace them to ensure they won't stick. Place about 1 teaspoon cream cheese mixture and 1 teaspoon hazelnut spread side by side in the middle of the round and lightly swirl the fillings.

Fold in 3 edges of the round to the center to form a triangle. Leave the top open and gently but firmly pinch the 3 points completely closed. Transfer to the prepared baking sheet. Repeat with remaining dough. Place pan in freezer for 20 minutes. Remove and brush the top and sides of the pastries with beaten egg white, then sprinkle lightly with coarse or regular sugar.

Bake for 16 to 20 minutes, until edges look dry and lightly browned. Remove from oven and let the pastries rest on the pan for 8 to 10 minutes before transferring to a wire rack. Enjoy right on the spot or cool completely and store in an airtight container for a couple of days.

Yield: 12 to 16 pastries (Dairy)

Sparkling Fruit Gelatinas

Gelatinas
2 tablespoons unflavored gelatin (about ³/₄ ounce; kosher gelatin can be found in kosher markets)

1 cup thawed frozen 100 percent juice frozen concentrate (such as apple raspberry)

1 generous tablespoon fresh lemon juice, about half a lemon

2 cups chilled Prosecco or other sparkling wine

2 cups fruit in bite-sized pieces (such as a mixture of blueberries and sliced strawberries)

Topping (optional)
¹/₂ cup mascarpone

2 tablespoons honey

Freshly grated nutmeg (optional)

Gelatin goes Italian and glam with a few simple but choice ingredients—Italian sparkling Prosecco wine, fruit, juice, and mascarpone. If you don't have individual glasses, simply plop the whole recipe into a nice serving bowl—it will taste just as good. Substitute whipped cream or nondairy whipped topping in place of the mascarpone topping if you like.

Sprinkle the gelatin over the juice concentrate and lemon juice in a small saucepan. Let stand 2 minutes. Whisk constantly over medium-low heat about 3 minutes until gelatin is completely dissolved.

Transfer to a large bowl and refrigerate until almost cool, 10 to 15 minutes. Stir in the Prosecco and refrigerate about 30 minutes, until the mixture is thicker but not set. Skim and discard any foam. Fold in the fruit and spoon gelatin into 6 or 7 wine glasses or dessert dishes. Cover and refrigerate until firm to the touch, at least 3 and up to 24 hours.

Before serving, combine the mascarpone and honey, and place a generous spoonful atop each portion. If using, dust with a sprinkle of nutmeg.

Yield: Seven ½-cup servings (Pareve without topping; Dairy with topping)

Keeping Kosher

At the heart of Jewish cooking are the laws of Kashrut, or keeping kosher. The basis for kosher law was established in the Torah, the first five books of the Bible. Over time, rabbis have interpreted those biblical rules and applied them to develop a specific set of guidelines for everything from what to eat and what it can be eaten with to how products should be packaged to how to ensure complete separation of dairy and meat products at home. Some American Jews observe these laws strictly, and some do not follow them at all. Others observe them to different degrees.

Strictly speaking, kosher animals must have split hooves and chew their cud. Kosher law forbids the following: pork, game animals, birds of prey, shellfish, and fish without fins and scales, such as catfish and monkfish. It also dictates that meat may not be eaten at the same time as dairy foods, such as cheese, butter, milk, yogurt, or ice cream. Eggs and fish are considered neutral and can be eaten either with meat or dairy foods.

To ensure that meat and dairy foods are kept strictly separate, kosher law mandates Jewish households keep two sets of dishes and cooking utensils, one each for meat and dairy meals. Furthermore, strict observance requires the purchase of only kosher meat, which has been raised and slaughtered according to the rabbinical guidelines for humaneness and cleanliness and under strict rabbinical supervision. Although kosher chicken and especially hot dogs can be more widely found, most kosher meat is available only from a kosher butcher. Grape products, namely wine and grape juices, must also be kosher—and that means wine-based liqueurs must be kosher, too. Some authorities require kosher certification for cheeses. Almost all other possible products are prepared and packaged under rabbinical supervision, and approved items are marked by symbols such as a "U" or "K" in a circle. Many kosher products can be purchased online. Fruits and vegetables do not require any special designation.

To complicate matters, Orthodox, Conservative, and Reform authorities do not always agree on the finer points of what is permissible under kosher law, and Ashkenazi Jews (from Eastern Europe) and Sephardi Jews (from Spain and Portugal) follow different rules, particularly at Passover. If you are keeping kosher, it's best to consult your rabbi for guidance. Several online resources provide comprehensive details, including the Orthodox Union (OU) Web site, oukosher.org, or the OK Kosher Certification Web site, Okkosher.com.

Throughout this book, I have labeled recipes as meat, dairy, or pareve (foods that are neither meat nor dairy and can be eaten with either one). Some recipes can be made either way, for example, a soup can be made with a vegetable broth and a cheese garnish or with chicken broth and no cheese. Other recipes give you the option of substituting margarine (nondairy) for butter (dairy) when you need a nondairy dish (although I always recommend opting for butter whenever possible because it tastes better and the results are more predictable). Note that typically the best-quality chocolate has some milk or milk solids in it, but some high-quality bittersweet chocolates are dairy-free. Dairy-free chocolate chips can be purchased at kosher markets.

I have done research and consulted authorities as I created these recipes to ensure that they could be prepared according to kosher rules. However, I am not an authority. Given the variance and many fine points of kosher rules, please check carefully to ensure the recipes adhere to your standards. And when in doubt, always check with your rabbi or other authority in your community.

I also realize that not everyone preparing recipes from this book will be keeping kosher. To make the recipes accessible to and successful for people not observing the dietary laws, occasionally recipes reference modifications that can be made if not keeping kosher.

Notes on Ingredients, Tools, and Spellings

Ingredients

Most recipes in this collection specify ingredients' types, sizes, amounts, and substitutions, but here are some general guidelines, tips, and recommendations:

- Butter—unsalted, unless otherwise noted; when a recipe calls for softened butter, the butter should be between 65 and 67 degrees.
- Eggs—large, and preferably organic cage-free.
- Vanilla—the best-quality pure vanilla extract you can find (except at Passover, when a kosher artificial vanilla flavoring is required).
- Sugar—granulated, unless otherwise noted.
- Salts—kosher salt is called for often. Note that different brands of kosher salt measure differently from one another and from regular table salt. I measured amounts using Morton kosher salt (1 teaspoon regular salt is equivalent to 1½ teaspoons Morton kosher salt).
- Dairy Substitutes—oil or margarine for butter; soy or coconut milk for milk; and nondairy whipped topping (or kosher-for-Passover nondairy whipping cream at Passover) for whipped cream.
- Lard—be aware that rendered pork fat (not kosher!) is sometimes used in refrigerated premade pie dough and biscuits and canned refried beans.
- Bread—check ingredients on packaged breads, because some use milk, and nondairy bread is required for kosher cooking of recipes that call for bread and meat, like meatloaf and meatballs.
- Broth v. Stock—authorities differ; for this book, I refer to stock as the liquid used as a foundation for a soup and broth as the liquid in a more finished and seasoned form as well as what you buy at the store in cans or cartons.

Tools

Most of the recipes in this book can be made using a kitchen stocked with basic tools, pans, and equipment. A large food processor or standing mixer is not necessary. Here are the tools that I find very helpful:

- An inexpensive handheld electric mixer for mixing batters, whipping cream, and so forth.
- A blender for pureeing soups, hummus, and such. Although not necessary, I've come to love using a handheld immersion blender for quickly pureeing soups right in the pot.
- A citrus juicer (manual or electronic) for quickly squeezing fresh lemon, lime, and orange juice.
- A microplane grater for quick and easy zesting of lemons and oranges.
- An instant-read thermometer for ensuring that dishes with meat or eggs have cooked enough to kill any potentially harmful bacteria.
- A candy or deep-fry thermometer for monitoring oil temperature so you can keep it in the proper (and safe) range for deep-frying.
- A pizza stone for even browning of breads and pizzas; a small peal is also handy.
- A small one- or two-cup food processor to make quick and easy work of finely chopping small quantities of items such as nuts or olives.
- A potato ricer for fluffy mashed potatoes and light gnocchi.
- Parchment paper for free-release and even browning of baked goods and easier handling of sticky ingredients.
- A light-colored baking sheet for baking cookies and other baked goods evenly.
- A garlic press for getting fresh garlic from whole clove to recipe-ready with just a squeeze.
- A meat mallet for pounding chicken breasts to an even thickness; also handy for pounding chocolate, candies, or cookies to bits for baking.

Spellings

Because Hebrew words do not translate directly to the Roman alphabet, there are many approaches to spelling certain words, often varying as to how different authorities interpret the letter combinations phonetically. You'll see matzah, matzoh, and matzo, for example. For the spelling of Hebrew words in this book, I usually deferred to the style guide of the United Jewish Communities (the predecessor of The Jewish Federations of North America).

Acknowledgments

When you've been working on a book as long as I have this one, you feel like thanking everyone you know for surely it has been a cumulative effort of guiding hands, good advisers, encouraging words, game and honest recipe testing and tasting, and the sharing of resources, recipes, tips, experiences, and insights. I appreciate every one of you and all that you've lent me on this journey.

There are those who I owe an even greater debt of gratitude

Sandra and Berney Thompson, my mom and dad, for raising me and making me the person I am today, and my mom for her patience, kindness, and openness in the kitchen and in life.

My brother Brian for being my very first recipe taster back when I was barely tall enough to reach the stove (sorry, but someone had to do it), and Brian and the rest of my family for being guinea pigs all through the years for concoctions of various sorts.

Daryl's parents, Gloria and David Friedman, for welcoming me to their lives with such warmth and enthusiasm and for embracing my cookbook endeavor.

Nita DiNenna for being more sister than cousin-in-law and for testing more recipes than anyone and for giving helpful feedback.

Lisa Resnick, one of the best editors I know, for reading the manuscript and reviewing designs multiple times, kindly but firmly pushing me to refine the copy and photography, and always being there as a sounding board.

Rabbi Avis Miller, someone for whom I have many things to thank, but for here, for reviewing an early version of the manuscript and recipes with an eye toward keeping the spirit and letter of the laws of kashrut.

Victoria Rapoport for her cheerful willingness from day one to test recipes, refer resources, and even lend her serving pieces for recipe photography.

Dan and Maxine Rapoport (Victoria's parents)—Dan, for reading some early sample chapters and sharing insights on cookbook publishing, and Maxine for sharing her delicious brisket recipe.

Nita Congress for helping find editorial professionals when I needed help and her support for this cookbook idea from the first time she heard about it.

Richard Peabody for giving the manuscript a thorough, honest critique. And for liking some of the recipes enough that he didn't want to send the hard copy back to me.

Steve Waxman for creating early designs and helping me think about how I wanted the book to look.

Lois Baron for copyediting the manuscript and recipes.

Laurie Wilkison for feedback on the design and final editorial reviews and proofreading that helped me get the manuscript over the finish line.

Josie Mani for reviewing early versions of the manuscript and recipes and making me and my ideas feel loved even in the roughest states.

Ron Gilbert for testing my brownie recipe and being the first person to serve one of my original recipes to me at a dinner party.

Gloria Robbins for always asking for "more recipes" to make, brightening my day with her warm reports back, and reminding me of the connections we make through shared foods.

Amy Hall for creating the index on a tight deadline.

Lucy Pope for her artistic eye and flexibility and beautiful design and layout of this book.

And saving the most important for last ... Daryl, thank you—which does not seem like a big enough phrase—for every. amazing. thing. But, especially, for your patience, optimism, humor, and insightfulness and your reviews of the stories and tastings of the recipes (many times over). And most of all for being my inspiration and life's love—this book simply would not have happened without you.

Bibliography

Amster, Linda, ed. *The New York Times Passover Cookbook*. New York: William Morrow and Company, 1998.

Beranbaum, Rose Levy. *The Cake Bible*. New York: William Morrow and Company, 1988.

Bittman, Mark. *How to Cook Everything*. New York: Macmillan, 1998.

Corriher, Shirley O. *Cookwise*. New York: William Morrow and Company, 1997.

Garten, Ina. *The Barefoot Contessa Cookbook*. New York; Clarkson Potter/Publishers, 1999.

————. *Barefoot Contessa Parties!* New York: Clarkson Potter/Publishers, 2001.

Goldman, Marcy. *A Treasury of Jewish Holiday Baking*. New York: Doubleday, 1998.

Goldstein, Joyce. *Cucina Ebraica: Flavors of the Italian Jewish Kitchen*. San Francisco: Chronicle Books, 1998.

Hazan, Marcella. *Essentials of Classic Italian Cooking*. New York: Alfred A. Knopf, 1992.

Kancigor, Judy Bart. *Cooking Jewish*. New York: Workman Publishing, 2007

Machlin, Edda Servi. *The Classic Cuisine of the Italian Jews I* (Revised Edition). New York: Giro Press, 1993.

————. *The Classic Cuisine of the Italian Jews II*. New York: Giro Press, 1992.

Madison, Deborah. *Vegetarian Cooking for Everyone*. New York: Broadway Books, 1997.

Nathan, Joan. *Jewish Cooking in America*. New York: Alfred A. Knopf, 1998.

————. *The Foods of Israel Today*. New York: Alfred A. Knopf, 2001.

Recipe Index

Made in the USA
Charleston, SC
05 February 2013